grand-daughter Anu Hewett-Spurr aged 6 years

Temporal House
books that empower

Published by Temporal House
Sydney, Australia
www.temporalhouse.co

Text and copyright © Peter Schmidt, 2022

All rights reserved. No part of this publication may be reproduced, distributed, or transmitted in any form or by any means, including photocopying, recording, or other electronic or mechanical methods, without the prior written permission of the publisher, except in the case of brief quotations embodied in critical reviews and certain other non-commercial uses permitted by copyright law.

First Printing, 2022

ISBN: 978-0-6450587-1-0

Table of Contents

Frontispiece: Acknowledgements .... i - iv

Foreword 1-8

SECTION A: MEMORIES 9-134

Odyssey 9-66
    Part III: The End of Innocence 9-40
    Part I: Emigration to Canada 41-46
    Part II: Canada and the European Grand Tour 47-66

Childhood 67-82

The Melded Family 83-104
    Family Secrets: 86
    Happy 50th Birthday, Michael: 88
    Wishing on the Same Bright Star: 90
    May the Light Shine on the Ones I Love: 91
    Butterfly Kisses: 93
    Another Romantic Story: 97
    The Grandchildren: 101

The Jobs 105-134

SECTION B: VIGNETTES 135-264

Frontispiece: Acknowledgements

Siblings

I would like to start by acknowledging the benefit of growing up in a large family of kids – something I share with Ann. While she shows clear signs of the 'eldest child' of the five, I guess I am a classic example of 'Malcolm in the Middle'!

We don't get together very often now, but one such occasion was elder sister Dorothy's 80th Birthday. Here we are in order after Dorothy on the left: Bro John, myself, Mary and Lois. I have devoted a whole chapter to ***Childhood***.

Frontispiece

The Melded Family

Ann and the family have played an enormous support role but, much more than that, just in being a constant source of joy and pride – the *raison d'etre* underpinning the entire story narrated in these pages. How fortunate Ann and I are to have a wonderful melded family, in chronological order: Michael Schmidt, Michael Spurr, Annie Schmidt and Samantha Spurr and their partners De Arnne, Pam, Joe and Ben. See the chapter: **The Melded Family.**

But it gets better. We started with a run of five grandsons and then a run of four granddaughters. Again, see chapter: **The Melded Family.**

Friends

Life-long friends like Roger and Virginia Nairn (Des, Libby and Clare), Geoff and Judy Washington, Trish and Ian Mackintosh (John, Luke and Ranae), Simon Berger, Margie and Ian McKay (Ella), Zue Ghani, Pam Bakhtir, Mike Berrell and Marianne Gloet, Peter Kavanagh, Lincoln Holland and Rhonda, and Konrad and Ann-Marie Bussler (and my godson Jan) have played a part in this narrative too.

Though we may have found ourselves in different countries or cities, in spirit we have never really been far away from each other confirmed by the ease at which we can reconnect when the occasion arises.

Frontispiece

The joy and influence that this group of close friends have given include the following examples:

- Geoff and Judy Washington's profound support without which there would not have been a Michael and Annie Schmidt at all (see *Odyssey Part III*)
- Libby Nairn and Annie Schmidt were such firm friends in their teenage years that they vowed, that when they grew up, if they had daughters, Libby would name hers Annie and Annie would name hers Libby – and they did!
- Ella McKay calls Ann her "Second Mum"
- Ann and I have been encouraging Simon Berger into the Prime Ministership for the last thirty years
- Luke and Ranae honoured me with the thrill of proposing the toast to the Bride and Groom at their wedding
- Desmier Nairn, not too reluctantly it seems, offered Michael Schmidt his first kiss at our house in Aranda. We surprised her with this photograph at her 21st Birthday Party

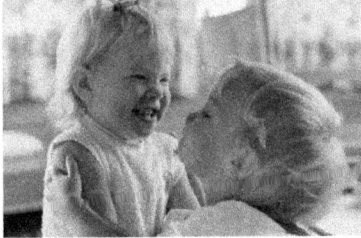

Frontispiece

Daughter Ann-Marie Schmidt (Annie) was named after Ann-Marie Bussler. In 2017, Ann and I visited Busslers and their son Jan (my godson) and wife Danielle.

The chapters **in the first section** of the memoire deal with subject matter which, being a little 'heavy' in parts, requires somewhat lengthy treatment. Also I have abandoned strict chronological order so that I can tell the tale as I think it should be told. However, I have named locations and dates where necessary.

Even though some of the stories narrated here are of acute embarrassment to me, I think that they need to be told especially to the family so that they can see some of the context around who we are and where we have come from.

I am acutely conscious of my own limited attention span when reading in bed. Within a few pages, my eyes glaze over and I enter the 'land of nod'. For this reason, I have transitioned from the first section into **a second section built around some vignettes**, in the style of short stories, each no more than a few pages in length.

I do hope you enjoy at least some of this!

Foreword

75 was a looming milestone – enough of a target to inspire launching an endeavour such as this. However, the motivation dissolved in our move to Sydney and the attendant real estate manoeuvres which swamped the time necessary for reflection. So only now, five years later in my eightieth year, am I able to return to this endeavour.

An Accounting Exercise: Your TWO Asset Vaults
Often called upon to give the 'keynote' speech at Orientation and Graduation, I am conscious of a huge responsibility. The students might actually remember what you say on occasions such as these!

I can clearly remember what the Vice-Chancellor of the University of Queensland said one February day in 1959 as we eager undergraduates congregated in the open grassed courtyard enclosed by the magnificent sandstone cloisters: "Each of you are the one selected from the forty of your classmates to make it into the University of Queensland. **Of you, much is expected**".

Those last five words still ring in my ears. Several of my contemporaries certainly met the challenge: David Malouf, Quentin Strachan (Bryce), Mr Justice Ian Hanger and the 'colourful identities' Mungo McCallum and Max "The Axe" Moore-Wilton, amongst others. So this memoire is, in a sense, an accounting exercise.

Phillip Adams in his piece in *The Australian* (Sept 19-20, 2015) related his words to the University of Newcastle students at a recent

Graduation Ceremony. He spoke of two vaults that each of us have. Bill Gates, for instance, may have $100 billion in one of his vaults but his second vault – the one that contains his days left on planet Earth – may have a meagre 10,000 days left. He is, after all, a 60-year-old.

Phillip had pointed this out to Kerry Packer after his near-death experience, warning him that he may have had a meagre 120 months left in the vault. As it happened, Kerry Packer did last an extra 5 years over and above that, but no amount of cash in the 'cash vault' could extend what was left in his 'days-left vault' any further.

Phillip pointed out to the University of Newcastle graduands that their 'days-left vault' is full to over-flowing, so he encouraged them: "Get stuck into your lives. There's not a moment to lose".

Accounting at age 67. at my 50th High School Graduation Reunion

The 2008 Reunion for the 50th Anniversary of my high school graduation was an occasion for accounting for the days spent and the days left. This was the entry I put into the commemorative almanac produced for the occasion.

Plus Ultra: **Ever Higher**

Headmaster Bill Lohe was right about insisting that my choice of science-based subjects be balanced by my continuing studies in History and German. Ten years later, during a year criss-crossing Europe, his point was underlined.

Foreword

The Maths, Chemistry and Physics, that you my classmates might remember me for, had proven their importance too. Just ten years from my St Peters graduation, they had underpinned a career that was financially successful enough to allow me to take a whole year off from my IBM job without any income – enough to enable me to buy a brand new fitted-out campervan and 'discover' Europe. It was there that I fully grasped why Bill Lohe had insisted that I would also study History and German.

Too bad the History lessons did not extend to Iran and Afghanistan. Far too bravely, I had extended the European Grand Tour to culminate in an overland Asian adventure. Almost ten years to the day that we left St Peters, it was all about to come to a shuddering full stop in tribal Afghanistan.

Was it the communication skills we had learned at school or the ability to think quickly or the intercession of a larger force that we also learned to respect at St Peters? Few have escaped being held down by a mob, when a massive rock had already been raised above their head by a band of men, shafts of mid-day sun piercing down behind the rock – but escape I did.

That experience did not quench my thirst for travel and adventure – a lifestyle ably supported by an academic career that took me to the Commonwealth Secretariat in London, University of Waterloo in Canada and Monash University in Malaysia totalling 50% of my career spent abroad.

Foreword

And my career continues today, developing MBAs in Melbourne "Australia's European City" and finally transferring to Sydney. With Australian academic salaries now an international embarrassment, it will be a while yet before I can say: "The King is in the Counting House counting all his money, the Queen is in the Parlour eating bread and honey". But I wouldn't want it any other way.

The next big milestone at age 70: 5th January 2011
To mark the biblical 'three score years and ten' milestone, the entire melded family travelled to South Australia and took up residence in the heritage-listed Mr Lofty railway station in the idyllic Adelaide Hills. This moment in time records four grandsons and no granddaughters from the ultimate tallies of five and four respectively.

Foreword

The station has been converted to encompass five en-suite bedrooms and, given its location abutting the main interstate railway track between Melbourne and Adelaide, it is securely enclosed from the platform by a sturdy picket fence.

Imagine the excitement eighteen times a day when, on the call "Train!", grandchildren (and oldies too) raced to the picket fence to view the express train roaring through the station! We were not the only ones excited. The location attracts train-spotters, replete with cameras and sound equipment, from all over the country.

The milestone at age 75: 5th January 2016

In the lead up to my Birthday, Ann and I had 'worked' ten days at the Conrad Hilton Resort in Nusa Dua. But we had thoughtfully forward-planned an escape to a resort to unwind at the end of the ten days of 'work'. We waved at our colleagues as our driver whisked us away from Nusa Dua for the drive to Ubud.

We started to relax arriving at the resort at about 2:30 pm with enough time to quickly settle in and hit the shops, as you do! Atypically, Ann seemed more interested in exploring the resort and the swimming pool in particular.

Around 4:00 pm, I noticed a small group of Aussie kids and I even remarked "They look a lot like our grandkids!" And who should leap forward in the best-kept surprise party I have ever had: Annie, Gary, Zander, Libby and Avi. They had flown up from Sydney- a top-secret mission coordinated by Annie and Ann.

Foreword

Resort guests around the pool were also astounded. They thoughtfully offered to film the re-enactment seen here.

The milestone at age 80: 5th January 2021

Surprise breakfast, a Zoom link-up with the entire melded family and a family trip to *RASCALs* Lodge in Jindabyne were the highlights that we managed despite lock-downs which, sadly, stopped our Melbourne friends from celebrating with us. The venue has special significance as, years ago, I had served as Rascal Lodge President.

Celebration dinner around the table at the Lodge

And here is the super-thoughtful present given to me from the family which matches nicely with our car's numberplate!

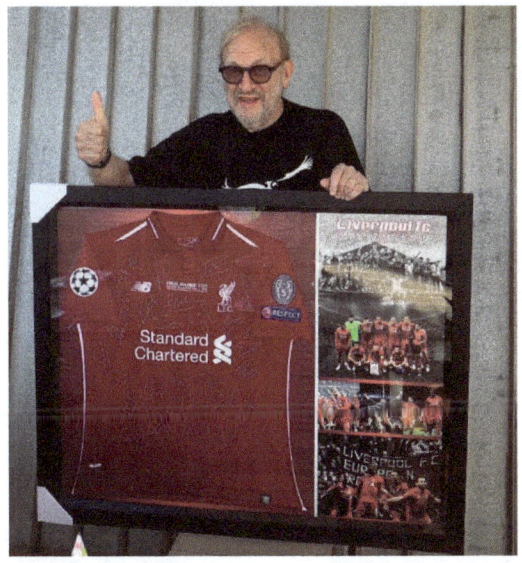

Foreword 8

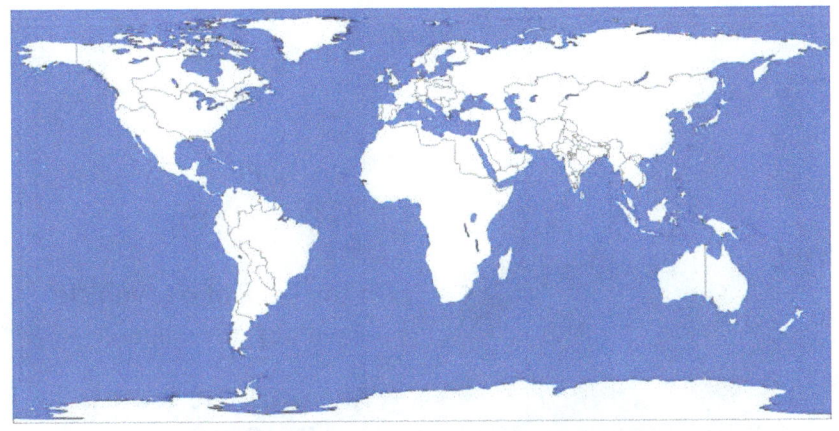

A round-the-world adventure in three parts:
Part I: From Australia to Canada; Part II: From Canada to the Europe;
Part III: From Europe to Australia
But narrated in non-chronological order

An Odyssey

Part III: The End of Innocence

Part I: Emigration to Canada

Part II: Canada and the European Grand Tour

Odyssey Part III: The End of Innocence

On the back of our vehicle we put our slogan:

AROUND THE WORLD IN 1080 DAYS

And that's just about right. Three years equals 1095 days and we were about 15 days short of that!

Part III: The End of Innocence
Asian Highway: London to Bombay, Nov-Dec 1968

The location is the tribal area of western Pakistan just beyond the Khyber Pass. This is a true story, but if what follows seems unbelievable, watch the movie *Argo* and it will give you a small taste of what this is all about.

The first stone sinks sickeningly into the windscreen. It sinks in sickeningly as if it were a blow to my stomach. So this stuff about the car as an extension of the persona is true. I guess a simple collision of cars would have been enough to have proven that. But this is no time for such reflection.

Would the laminated screen be enough to hold these 4kg stones raining in on it now?

Slow down, low gear. Keep pressing the Kombi van through the tumult – must not kill anyone – or we are all dead. This press through the violent angry throng is physical too, as if pushing through an angry football mob coming towards us – 200 of them.

The damage is fearful, our 'dream machine', which had been our home as well as our transport these last eight months, has lost most of its windows by now. The thudding of the stones against the metal is deafening.

To have been pressed to a halt would be fatal for us (cue in the footage of the crew of the *Argo* visiting the Teheran bazaar). But, at last, we are through – a miracle – a driving triumph. Speed up now and get the hell out of here!

We look at each other as we speed down the road. I expect some thanks for a daring 'Indiana-Jones-style' driving escapade, but then again I am the one responsible for all of this. Perhaps I should be apologizing.

An anxious look in the rear-view mirror confirms that we are drawing away from the mob now running after us. Our (motorized)

Odyssey Part III: The End of Innocence 13

technology has saved us again – but a lot closer this time. Many times in the last 30 days we had sped off after an intrusive photograph. In the Turkish highlands a tribesman had actually run after us with an axe. We easily outran him – a classic getaway, exhilarating really! A bit of fun. But this is different somehow, much more serious, and the damage is severe. Maybe those warnings about the Khyber Pass region were true.

Len Hornich, camping with us on the border last night had shown us his mini-arsenal of weapons. For the first hour this morning, we had followed him in convoy over the border for safety, but he was long gone now – we were too slow – all those photographs!

Now it dawns on us that it must have been the photographs. It was women this time bearing loads on their heads. But what's new? What's different? They must have had a way of alerting ahead as we were making our exhilarating getaway. An Afghanistan version of the Swiss yodel, perhaps. Enough time for them to have organized this 'reception committee' in the next village ten minutes down the track.

Brief Reflection

Time now to reflect on the damage. So the bad luck of a broken windscreen some months earlier in Vienna, was not such bad luck after all since its laminated replacement, badly deformed by the battering, had held up much better than the crystal glass original that it replaced would have done. The windscreen, badly deformed, pressed in with many hits in line with the driver, sparked a chilling realization of what they were trying to do – take out the driver. Those stones had been well directed.

Pat has been hit by a stone that has penetrated a non-laminated side window and is being attended by Judy in the back seat of the Kombi. As the driver, I am vomiting sick from the psychological shock of each hit on the vehicle. It is as if each was a hit in my stomach. That the vehicle could have become such an extension of my persona is not so surprising considering that, apart from it being a considerable, loved asset, it has been our home as well as our transportation for the last eight months.

Odyssey Part III: The End of Innocence 15

Continuing on…..

We drive in silence now – too stunned to talk. We are each in our private world. None of us has any words. A car honks – it's an old Mercedes behind us. We've seen lots of these on route from Germany to someone out east with money. This one is in even more of a hurry than us. I move across to let him pass.

Ten minutes have passed since we escaped the village throng. The road is a first-class elevated highway, a gift of American aid. It's better than the previous 200 miles of road which were a gift of Soviet aid. Despite the fact that we are in a desert, this must be a flood plain for the melting snow from the surrounding mountains, because there is a bridge coming up. And that's when I see the old Mercedes parked across the elevated highway lanes on the bridge. We're blocked. Nowhere to go. And six armed tribesmen out of the car coming towards us firing at us. This must be the execution squad.

I screech the van to a halt before we get into close range. Trapped on this elevated highway, five feet above the surrounds with an execution squad coming at us from the front and screaming mob who can't be too far behind us, I have no choice but to slam the vehicle into reverse and pull a tight three point turn and head back down the road in a search for a side road before the pincers movement closes on us.

Having a gun seriously pointed at me for the first time in my life is one thing, but this feeling of being option-less in a rapidly closing trap will cause me to wake up screaming for ten years after.

We're trapped but we find voice now. Geoff remembers that somewhere in the last five minutes or so since the village there was a turn-off road – wasn't it a veterinary hospital or something? With some high speed reversing and a lightening three-point turn, we are dashing back to find the turn-off where we might find some United Nations workers – that's the plan – as we have no other realistic choice.

We get to the turn-off just before the trap closes from both ends. As we drive up the 200 yards to the Vet Hospital, I have temporary relief from the 'closing trap' feeling that was to haunt me. Nothing I have ever experienced can compare to the feeling of being a trapped animal.

But the relief is temporary. We can see both ends of the trap closing on us down that 200-yard side road and…the hospital is deserted! I feel a sense of resignation as we wait briefly for the inevitable. A strange calm comes over me, almost a feeling of relief.

Geoff grabs our only 'weapon' - our fire extinguisher. Showing presence of mind, he has got our wives out of the vehicle. I do nothing, staying seated in the driver's seat, winding up the only window not broken, locking my door, and waiting out the two minutes of calm before the storm which is about to engulf me.

The storm breaks with the smashing of that window and the wrenching back of the driver's door on it hinges – the locking of it to no avail, merely delaying proceedings for a few seconds.

Outnumbered and overpowered, I don't struggle accepting what is happening with a sense of resignation until... Suddenly I realize that the method of my death is to be by ritual stoning. Held to the ground now with the screaming throng around me, I see the huge boulder held aloft by four or five of them silhouetted against the sun. I see the sun glinting behind the boulder.

It was about feelings

Writing this years later from the notes I made at the time I can say that, if anything, that climatic paragraph is a mastery of understatement but only because of the limitation of any words to describe what it was all about. It was about feelings. It was about time that seemed suspended. It was about my actions - totally reflex, not thought-out, to be endlessly 'replayed' and critically self-evaluated with pride or disgust. But mostly it was about traumatic feelings of powerlessness, of feeling like a trapped animal, of feeling guilty for getting my wife and closest friends into this, and of feeling resigned to the inevitable. All of that took fully ten years to resolve.

I recall a sense of the waste of all those years of education, of growing up, of civilizing influence of culture. All of this was, in a moment, to be torn away. The naked animal facing its death – and it was to be a horrible death.

Can anyone speak English!

Not so smart now, stripped down to the deepest level of personal resources, I find a primæval scream to the mob, in English: *"Can anyone speak English?"*

The stone is lowered! The single tribesman who can speak faltering English presses forward to the inner circle of the throng that surrounds me. I am suddenly on my feet! The tribe is arguing loudly. "What do they want?" I scream. I scatter whatever American dollar currency I have in my wallet - a plan to distract the mob, but the plan seems to fail. *"The car, take it, take what's left of it, take it. Take it all, just let us go!"*

I look at he who is our only hope and he motions as if to take a photograph. *"Take the camera!"* ...... No? But then he motions as if to remove film from a camera.

Now, for the first time, it dawns on me what has triggered this horror. I quickly strip the film from the camera in full view of the mob. At this point Geoff seems to be coming back towards our vehicle with the distraught Judy and Pat. The mob is arguing. They seem not to be satisfied.

Something tells me that the film has captured their souls. I had assaulted them, almost as if they had been raped. The punishment to be meted out could only be appropriate in a context such as that.

And then I have a blinding flash of reason. Weren't they now doing something to 'our women' as bad, or even worse, than that which I had done to 'their women'? I frame it in simple English, screaming the telling argument with all of my being.

Confusion. Pandemonium. Some of the mob relent but some want to restart where we had left off. Our 'friend' screams: "Go!" We jump in the car – a volley of shots pierces the steel shell of the car. I agonize over the jerry cans full of petrol on the roof rack of the van. One bullet, at any stage of this siege, would convert it into a giant Molotov Cocktail.

We rush back up the side road to re-join the highway. In the rear-view mirror half of the tribe is running after us menacingly again. Speed to the bridge. The clapped-out Mercedes is gone. We're through! However, I can't keep my eyes off the rear-view mirror. [It is some days before it occurs to me that this persistent habit is making me sick. Is this paranoia?]

Escape?

We have escaped with minor flesh wounds from bullets and glass apart from Pat who will need stitches. One of the boulders has penetrated a side window and struck her head. The towel is soaked with blood already.

I'm driving like a maniac hardly looking at the road, eyes fixed on the rear view mirror. A UN Hospital appears, it's probably a half an hour now since we have sprung the trap. We are met by an English doctor who presses us to vamoose immediately! For him to even lift a finger to help us would result in his hospital being burned down, he says. They already know about us and about what has happened, and we are about as popular as lepers. We are shocked at the efficiency of the primitive communication systems…more Afghan yodelling through the hills, perhaps? Peshawar, he says – just three hours away – they will help you there. We have no choice. I must drive – a man possessed – eyes fixed on the rear view mirror.

Sitting in the hospital in Peshawar, I get the shakes. I cannot accompany Pat into surgery. Geoff and Judy do that – and they are very caring. Actually, I want to be alone – I know I am not 'quite right'. I sit there shaking, unable to acknowledge any form of 'weakness'. It just doesn't fit my personal self-image.

Such was my state of mind that memories of what followed are sketchy. It would take us time to complete the drive to Bombay where we had an owner's cabin booked so we could accompany the car shipping to Sydney. But for me, time was lost in a time warp brought about by what I now know was excessive internalization, simple worry. But there won't be a 'solution' there. In fact, the opposite is true - one must externalize – talk it out. But I didn't do that. Many times in the next weeks as we continued our travels, people I met said: *"You must snap out of it, Peter"*.

A visit to our High Commission in Islamabad to lodge an official complaint, was one occasion I was forced to 'snap out of it' and verbalize.

Odyssey Part III: The End of Innocence 21

There is an official record of that visit. I remember them saying:

You're alive so just what is your complaint? They let you go, didn't they? Last week, they burned a Red Cross van, but they let you go! Things happen up there in the Pass. They <u>never</u> let them go. How the hell did you talk your way out of it, they ask. And how can we then complain when they let you go. Didn't you know these are tribal areas that even the Pakistan Government does not control. Diplomatic relations have improved lately (and further complaint now will only set things back, they implied).

As we exited the Australian High Commission, we suffered the first of many mobbings. The state of our vehicle acted like a magnet. It telegraphed that we had been in some kind of trouble. Maybe, they had even heard about it. Each mobbing begins to look more and more like a re-run of that tribal mob that had trapped us.

Geoff arranges to get all the car windows fixed while I have convinced myself that what I have to do is to think things through. I'm still doing a bit of driving, staring at that rear view mirror. I'm so busy thinking things through that I don't talk much now, but my mind is racing. I don't sleep for days on end, but it gives me more time to think without disturbance.

Deterioration

My travelling companions watch me a lot now ever since I lost control of my bladder one day. In fact, they have not realized yet that a huge responsibility has passed to them. I have become incapable of looking after my own health. In cases like this, the onus shifts to those around you, and they must act quickly in your best interests.

People we meet seem to be annoyed with me: "Pull yourself together", they'd say. I confess that's exactly what I think whenever I encounter a reprobate even today. However, thinking back to my own experience, what the sufferer really needs must come from outside of themselves. They need help.

Sometimes we are treated as drug addicts on a 'bad trip' - Hippy Aussies having established a reputation on the Asian Highway.

One day, I escape from the compound where we sleep and walk back along the big highway. There is a big truck coming towards me, but I realize that suicide would invalidate my insurance. I want Pat to be well cared for. It feels that I won't have to hang on too much longer for death and she will qualify for the insurance.

They won't let me drive anymore now. One of my three travelling companions is always watching me. Sometimes I have little fits and sometimes I hallucinate. That scares me a lot because I earn my living with my brain and my brain seems to be going bad. I really don't want to live anymore without this, my greatest asset, and I feel sad a lot now.

I get very upset in the presence of mobs even anyone with dark skin. I remember insulting a dark-skinned doctor to whom I have literally been dragged kicking and screaming. I escape when they are not watching and run like hell away from everybody. Geoff finds me eventually. They insist that I take some pills, they say that they will cure me. This is obviously a lie, so I refuse. The three of them hold me down – like the tribal mob had done – and force me to take the pills. I can't even understand why I am convinced that it is so important for me NOT to take the pills. I remember thinking that this is my last level of free will and I must not abandon that, so I must not take the pills. I hold them in my mouth and spit them out later!

We are in India now, and some nice people talk to me and seem concerned to help. I had absolutely refused to accept any help from the Australian consul as I knew any such approach would create a public record and there must be no blemish on the record if I am ever to make a comeback.

I wrestle mentally with a lot of energy thinking things through. It seems to go round and round. The circular ceiling fan in the hotel room at our beach resort in Bombay is driving me crazy – round and round. Years later, hearing the song *Windmills of your Mind*, I immediately knew what the writer had suffered. All of this seems to be linked to my breathing. I have become super-aware of my breathing – it is almost as if I have to make a conscious decision to take every breath. I have bouts of super-agitated behaviour, but I never get angry or violent. One night, I rush from the hotel room springing open the door of another room. I can't recall what I was looking for, if anything, but the stunned expressions on the faces of the Indian family who crouched at the end of their bed stays with me forever. I can't imagine how difficult I am making things for Pat, Judy and Geoff who had to smooth over such bizarre behaviour.

I yearn for the crutches of civilization – for some decent music to take my mind off my worries. Their radio is horrible.

Pat and I sit by the beach – Juju Beach littered with garbage. I have even forgotten how to play tic-tac-toe. That really scares me. I am now having bad headaches.

The Homecoming

Somehow, Geoff has managed to swap our super-desirable Owner's Cabin on the ship to someone who was glad to give us air tickets.

I don't remember much of the flight except that someone mentioned Kuala Lumpur (we were landing at K.L's original Sungi Besi aerodrome). By convoluted logic, I had interpreted this as: [Kuala = Koala = Pat] and [Lumpur = lump her = get rid of *him*]. Putting it together: *Pat, get rid of him!* I became very agitated about that!

I remember lights coming through a taxi window as we must have stayed in a hotel there. Then there were the Customs procedures in Singapore and Darwin. How Pat managed to get me through all that I will never know as none of us ever wants to talk about any of this.

Sometime later in the flight heading to Brisbane the full horror of the disastrous homecoming hits me. As all expatriates do, I had so much looked forward to that day and it was to have been a triumph. I just couldn't go through with it like this. I grabbed an umbrella and attacked the window of the 'plane with some force, breaking the inner of the double windows before they could restrain me. Pat and another person she knew on the 'plane managed to smooth all of this over somehow, drawing the window blind across the damage!

I remember seeing my mother, father brothers and sisters who met the 'plane and I was told later that they had been pre-warned. A good meal would go some way to fixing things, was the reaction of any good mother and so they drove us to their home. I remember sitting on the couch totally immobile and uncommunicative. It became very clear to my father that I needed hospital, and I am eternally grateful that they organized a very private hospital mental facility and Brisbane's top psychiatrist with WWII experience.

It was dark. All of a sudden the Afghans were outside the hospital; the tribal mob had caught up with me. I became very agitated and leapt out of bed. I remember the embarrassment when I realized that I had an erection.

One night, in the middle of the night, I rushed into the nurse's office and dialled 38 1756 – a number that I had not dialled in three years. It was my parent's home phone number. In the confusion, I remember feeling proud that I was able to remember the number. As I was taken back to bed, I realised that I was in Australia, not Afghanistan. I noticed a fully decorated Christmas tree outside my window.

I began to notice that there were other people in the ward and that I was the only one with a metal knife and fork at mealtimes. I had never been violent.

A doctor appeared and talked about my being silly nearly killing myself – it had been close, he said – and then he talked about hiding places – he said I had to come out of my hiding place.

It must have been some time later that I saw all my family around the bed looking down at me – just like lying on the ground with the big rock held above my head and the mob around me. I remember how sad they looked particularly wife Pat. But I also remember feeling as if I was the only one going on a train journey and it was going to be very lonely. They'd feel sad until the train pulled out and then quickly, they would all get over the departure.

Odyssey Part III: The End of Innocence

Another feeling I had was that the world was crashing around me, even closing in on me. In reality, it was I who was crashing – a classic illustration of the relativity principle. Bit like looking at that other train at the station – is it moving or is it our train that is moving.

I wish I didn't have these insights about death, but I discovered a lot that I wish I didn't know. I lost whatever faith I had in God. As one part of me observed my brain (personality) falling apart I grieved at the destruction. No good purpose could be served by that. A God would have stopped that happening.

Just as an Alzheimer sufferer's persona 'dies' slowly, mine had died quickly. But I also discovered that each of us 'lives' in others. I found out later that my very skilled psychiatrist gleaned pieces of my persona from each of my close family members and, as if solving a jig-saw puzzle, he pieced them together with me in sessions where I had been sensitized to suggestions by ECG. Yes, ECG! ECG saved my life, and for a few days I was totally unaware of all of this. As I gradually became aware, I became concerned that he should not give me any more such sessions – not fear of pain, but concern about the effects of electric currents on my brain. But he was a very skilled psychiatrist, and I need not have worried about that.

Many years later, I learned that Egyptians believe that the 'persona' lives on while ever we speak the name. For this reason, a disgraced pharaoh has their name removed from pyramids and *stelae*. And so, I do believe in this as a form of 'immortality' - of an immortal Winston Churchill, for instance.

Comeback?

Suddenly, reality returned. It was just like a regular hospital with me arguing with the doctor about wanting to go home. I had been in hospital just over seven days! My family, and I too, felt there had been a miracle. I was able to come back from the brink. Many never leave their 'hiding place' - their new 'reality'.

The doctor cautioned that, when I got out of hospital, I would find it hard going. He encouraged me to believe that I could make a comeback in an Australian environment. "You're good in this environment", he said. "It was only from the Afghanistan environment that you had retreated". "Imagine how hard it was for shell-shock soldiers to return to the very same environment from which they had retreated". "It will be easier for you, Peter", he said. "Why don't you finish off your second degree – the Economics degree that your family told me you had been working on?" [He is a very good doctor, isn't he?].

He warned me that I probably would not feel happiness again for as long as two years but that I *have* to believe that I will get there! And yes, it was hard; it was very, very hard: the lost confidence, the lost 'mojo' and the constant sadness.

But I knew I had a CV to protect if ever I was to make a full comeback. "Work on a farm for a while", he said! But I knew I could never do that. How would I ever explain such a thing – a glaring gap in my work record.

The way back

It was clear to me there was to be no sojourn on a farm for me even though my doctor had recommended it. I felt strongly that I must keep my CV intact. The doctor's focus was on the real issue: that the patient be intact.

It was Contract Bridge that was to be part of my pathway back. I have often joked that I would like to get back the ten years that I laboured to achieve Grand Master status in the Contract Bridge world. The occasional newspaper article about my exploits at the table, the achievement of interstate representative status at national tournaments, the interest of Frank Theeman's scouts for a paid 'career' on his team, all of that was not a good substitute for the PhD I should have been taking out at that time. But I needed the validation at the Bridge table to prove something to myself.

Then, there was also the other little matter of a condition that I now know to have been Post Traumatic Stress Disorder PTSD.

I was only able to emerge from all of this just short of my 40th year, in 1981 after completing my Masters at University of Waterloo in Canada. But it had been a 10-year setback to my career.

Pat could have abandoned me anywhere in Asia at any of the points where my behaviour had caused a disaster, but she stuck with me. Together with my family they got me to the A+++ medical care, which would not blemish my record. Also, she resumed work as the major breadwinner over the period of my recovery.

I don't think she liked the new persona much though and it ended in divorce eventually and I can't blame her for that even though I said, I would never leave her after what she had done to rescue me.

After just one week, I left hospital on tranquilizers, with a plan to protect my CV with part-time supply teaching! Needing more money than that, I was also able to get a job driving taxis, despite the tranquillizers!!! The plan was: part-time supply teaching in the government high school system for professional respectability and taxis to augment the funds.

It was in the supply teaching role where I was haunted by my old persona and I think it was then that I resolved, when I was able, that I would have to leave Brisbane, all old friends, all connections with my former persona. The problem was that, in the three years before leaving Australia, I had established a reputation as a successful teacher at the Grammar School. Brisbane is a small town and my reputation preceded me. My supply-school headmaster became aware of the mayhem in my classroom at his school and called me to the office. It's a bit harder in a government school, he said - my performance confirming his pre-conceived ideas. I could have said: *"Ever tried keeping discipline in a classroom while you are on massive doses of Largactil?"* I remember the day Armstrong set foot on the moon. Thank heavens for that, a TV was wheeled into my classroom, and we had peace for a while!

One day I was summoned to the Headmaster's office. Fearing the worst, I was astounded by his feigned warmth. He wanted to

Odyssey Part III: The End of Innocence

make sure I would attend speech night as I, along with him, was the only degree holder on staff. *"Bring the gown"*, he reminded me! I do feel a bit guilty about the poor kids I inflicted myself upon, but I justify it all by resort to the 'greater good', the 'big picture', my 'comeback scheme' which actually worked.

And you can see how I passed the Inspection by Inspector who visited Nashville High School. Though we have the proof here, this is *not* one of my proudest achievements.

It was interesting, despite all my care in keeping my CV clean with this 'cover story' of supply teaching to avoid the 'red flags' that a period of farm rehab would have raised, that about five years after taking that careful decision, during a high level ASIO clearance for a job that I had at the time, the Afghanistan 'incident' was blurted out by a senior person who obviously had been briefed. He was citing this as a great example of overcoming adversity to my great embarrassment. So, I guess not much misses ASIO.

I personally often wonder what I might have achieved had I not lost 10 years pursuing Contract Bridge instead of my PhD. It is, however, fatal to think like that – I decided never to use a disability as a crutch. I made that decision in 1969, to assiduously put all of this behind me and to walk away from my former persona and my former life and that would mean leaving all that behind in Queensland as soon as I was able to do so. It is for this reason that I haven't wanted to occupy the haunts of my former persona. Mr Justice Hanger, once a personal friend, might not even have recognized my new persona. Ever since, I have kept my distance.

And so, not twelve months after Afghanistan, I slid effortlessly, without embarrassing questions about any 'gaps' in my work-record, into *two* good job offers *out* of Queensland and that was very important to me.

Aftermath

It was five years before I could talk about this. I'm not sure whether the others have ever talked about this or ever will. I still feel responsibility for the trauma that my actions inflicted on the other three companions, though my doctor continuously stressed that I must not think like that. I talk about it now in the hope that this story, painful as it is for me, might help others.

I lost my naivety that day in Afghanistan – I lost my innocence in one fell swoop. Stripped of all layers, I was down to my very essence. If I have any pride, it is that I didn't give up, that we didn't have

Odyssey Part III: The End of Innocence

weapons (as no matter how many we would have killed we would have been killed too). I have pride that I used my wits to find a way out. Most of all, I am very proud of my comeback.

I learned a very important lesson that we all have our limits; we all have a breaking point, and it's vital to recognize when you are getting close to it. Don't underestimate PTSD, it may still be with me even now to some extent. There is another very big lesson in this too: We all have a massive responsibility to our loved ones around us, because the onus is on us to instigate treatment for them, even against their will, if we see the signs. One of the key symptoms of poor metal health is the inability of the sufferer to seek help. It is actually a sign of good mental health to seek help.

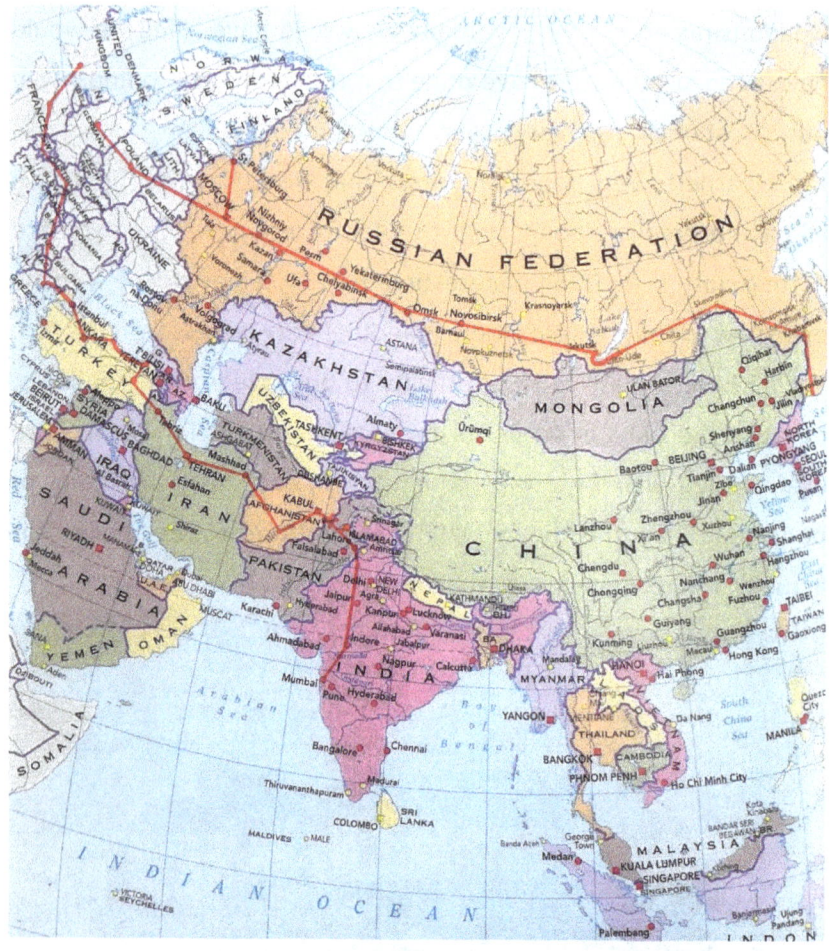

1968: The Asian Highway overland: London to Mumbai

1979: Trans-Siberian Railway: Nakhodka (USSR) to Berlin
[See *Vignette: Trans-Siberian Railway*]

A F F I D A V I T

I Peter Schmidt, (Passport No. G107852) of Brisbane Australia, make oath and say as follows:

On 25 November 1968 I was travelling with my wife Pat (a British citizen), Geoff and Judy Washington (both Australian citizens) in my car, a 1968 Vokkswagen Campervan, from Torkham, on the Afghanistan/Pakistan border, to Rawalpindi. We left Torkham at 7.30a.m. and at about 9.00a.m. had arrived on the outskirts of a village about 10 miles from Peshawar.

I stopped the car and got out to take a photograph of four women with large loads on their heads: one woman picked up a stone. I returned to the car and drove on. About one mile further, in the centre of the village, a large crowd had gathered, at what appeared to be a bus stop. They moved across the road to prevent us passing. I drove through the crowd at about 20m.p.h. Stones were thrown after us, one breaking the rear window striking Pat on the head rendering her momentarily unconscious.

About two miles further on we were passed by a car which then parked across a narrow bridge making it impassable. From this car about twelve armed men advanced towards us. Meanwhile I stopped our car, reversed at high speed before turning and driving back to the village where we thought we had seen a military establishment. We were, however, blocked by the mob coming from the centre of the village. We entered a side street which took us to a Vetinary Hospital. The mob (of about 200) followed. I remained in the car while the other three ran to the building. Geoff took with him a fire extinguisher which was our only weapon.

All windows in the car were then broken. I was pulled from the car and offered money which was refused. One man who seemed to have some authority mentioned the camera. Geoff, who had been forced at gun point from the room where the girls were, found our cameras. We took the film out and gave it to them. This seemed to quieten the crowd somewhat. Apart from the damage to the car and my Pentex camera (worth $200) we only lost a few articles. Some items were, in fact, handed back to us as we drove off.

Pat and Judy were joined by a few English speaking members of the hospital staff, including a doctor who took the girls to the car and advised us to try to make a break and see the political representative in the village. As we did not want to spend more time in that village we drove, without further incident, to Peshawar.

At Peshawar we notified the police who said there was little they could do as the village was in a tribal area. One policeman, however, took us to a mission hospital which was not anxious to help Pat for fear of the possible repercussions with the villagers, and which we did not think was of a very high standard. The policeman took us to the political representative of the village who was in Peshawar. We wished to have him guarantee that something would be done to quieten the village as we knew of other tourists travelling that way on the same day. He was sympathetic but thought we were threatening legal proceedings and asked us to make a formal complaint to him after Pat had been to hospital and he would investigate it. We did not make the complaint and decided to drive to Rawalpindi.

We arrived at about 3.00p.m. at a Military Hospital on the outskirts of Rawalpindi. The staff of this hospital were most helpful and the surgeon cleaned and stitched Pat's wound. We attempted to contact the Australian High Commission and finally reported the incident to Mr. A. R. Taylor.

It would seem that this whole incident stemmed from my attempt to photograph one of the local women. There was no warning, as far as I am aware, that this would be dangerous. Admittedly there is a sign at the border saying that no photography was allowed in the Khyber Pass but it was assumed this was because of military installations and anyway we were well clear of the Pass. Nor were we aware that we were in a tribal area.

Sworn at Rawalpindi in Pakistan on this day of 26th November, 1968, Before me Allan Robert Taylor, Third Secretary.

Affidavit sworn at Rawalpindi in Pakistan on this day of 26th November, 1968 Before me, Allan Robert Taylor, Third Secretary

25th November 1968

Without being too dramatic, it is not an exaggeration to highlight that date when it all could have ended in the Afghan-Pakistan border region. And for what? Not surprisingly, I have held very hard-boiled attitudes to Afghanistan ever since. Half-seriously, I have even advocated bombing it into oblivion arguing that there is no good thing there except spectacular desert/mountain scenery. These attitudes come from my lived experience.

Coping as a victim of barbarism

It was Christmas 1968, but I would not have known it but for the lights of a Christmas tree that I could see from my bed. The lights and the familiar image impinged upon my consciousness and may have triggered the first sane thoughts I'd had for weeks. Then I noticed the ward in this private hospital on Wickham Terrace emptying out. Nobody wants to be in hospital at Christmas time.

Earlier in 1968, Louis 'Satchmo' Armstrong had released his masterpiece *"What a Wonderful World"*. I remember hearing it from my hospital bed – *"I see skys of blue, red roses too... and I say to myself, What a Wonderful World"*. It meant a lot to me at the time, and I actually think it helped in my regaining my MOJO!

When I hear Teddy Tahu Rhodes' version of Leonard Cohen's *Hallelujah*, I experience a similar uplift!

Updating the Afghanistan Experience

I know a lot more *now* about what we were getting into in the Afghanistan-Pakistan border region. It is a lawless tribal area founded on poppies initially established by American traders in competition with British traders of Indian-grown opium.

The trade with China dates from the early-1800s and the British Opium Wars, one outcome of which was that the trade was legalized, and American traders needed to compete given the British stranglehold of the market.

Few American Defense members who had served in Afghanistan knew that their forebears had a role in all of this.

> I the Lord your God am a jealous God **visiting the iniquity of the fathers on the children to the third and the fourth generation** of those who hate me but showing steadfast love to thousands of those who love me and keep my commandments. Exodus 20:5–6

31st August 2021

In the lead up to the ill-chosen date of 11th September 2021 – the twentieth anniversary of 9/11 – Joe Biden, holidaying in Camp David, had the expression of a stunned animal caught in the headlights. I guess he *was caught* in the limelight of TV, stunned at the scene at Kabul airport which unfolded on the screen in front of him – a scene that should have been entirely predictable and planned for.

There were further indignities in store. On the actual anniversary date of 9/11, the Taliban raised the ISIS flag atop what had been the American Embassy in Kabul no doubt emboldening a generation of terrorists and embarrassing America and its allies.

There is no doubt that twenty years of effort had made Afghanistan a better place particularly for women, but one should not have been surprised that it so quickly reverted to what it had always been.

Odyssey Part III: The End of Innocence

The foregoing narrative was at the end of a three-year Odyssey. Let's go back now to the start of that story, **start-date 6th January 1966,** as we sailed through Sydney Heads at the beginning of a great adventure, full of hope and excitement. Two crucial friends in the foregoing narrative -Geoff and Judy Washington – were there too on P&O's *Oronsay* as we sailed away to North America.

We're heading out to the first port of call, Auckland. For those interested in shipping matters, the *SS Oronsay* rated at 28,000 tons.

A more interesting fact is that in 1960, six years earlier than our voyage to Canada, a famous two-year-old emigrated from U.K. to Australia on the *Oronsay*, ultimately to serve as an Australian Prime Minister: Tony Abbott.

Odyssey Part I: Emigration to Canada
Voyage to North America, Jan 1966; First trip abroad

The quintessential Australian view – the gateway in and out of Australia – who could resist such an open door? That view to the horizon and the open sea beyond begged to be explored at every visit to the beach even from my earliest childhood.

Here, on the **6th January 1966**, just a day after my 25th Birthday, began

my very first exploration of what lay beyond on a ship not unlike this one passing through Sydney Heads.

But unlike this trip, ours was much more than a cruise or even an exploration sortie. Ours was an immigration story - one to rival, perhaps, those stories of potato famine Irish immigrants heading to the riches of Buenos Aires or to the freedoms of the new world epitomized in the welcome from New York's Statue of Liberty.

Now, sitting on our balcony 55 years later, watching cruise ships passing through the Heads, it is interesting to reflect on how the hopes of our close group of six on the *Oronsay* passing the Heads *en route* to Canada actually panned out!

We were truly so, so brave. Or was it the confidence of youth and a total ignorance of risk! Sadly, however, by the end of the three-year odyssey begun on this day, we were to understand risk as a lived experience.

No words can describe the confidence and hopes that propelled our fearless group out through the Heads into 'the big, bad world'. Excited anticipation masked the risks we had already taken:

- Each of us had resigned from a safe well-paid job
- Each of us had paid a considerable sum for our fares but, in total cost terms, the opportunity cost of **no income** for the six weeks of the voyage overwhelmed the cost of the fares
- None of us had a job lined up at the other end, though we all had ideas and hopes

Odyssey Part I: Emigration to Canada

[The photo? Geoff and Judy; Peter and Pat; Sue and Trevor]

Over the six weeks that it took to cross the Pacific we really got to know each other's hopes. Summarizing the hopes of our group of six: One was fairly sure of a teaching job in Canada; one was hoping for a library opportunity; one hoped to break from teaching and start a business career; one hoped for a physiotherapist position at a Canadian hospital; one hoped for a graduate business secretary position; and one hoped for an opportunity to develop his career in architecture.

All of us were well armed with impressive qualifications and CVs. Our varied academic and personal interests soon showed with our dining table group emerging as virtually unbeatable in the trivial pursuit competition which attracted some 700 of our fellow passengers each evening.

SS Oronsay had become our home: we loved the coloured streamers as we departed each port; we loved the bands that greeted and farewelled us from each port; the summons to the deck for the passage through Puget Sound, so beautiful that it brought tears to the eyes; the energy of the rendition of *"California here I come"* as we left Vancouver. The Captain offered a free continuation beyond Vancouver to San Francisco and Los Angeles. We even got to visit a relatively new *Disneyland,* just 25 years old at that time. It was quite a wrench back to reality to leave our 'home' in Los Angeles.

The jolt back to reality was palpable arriving as we did in the middle of a Canadian winter - a profound contrast from the Australian mid-summer and balmy Pacific waters that we had left albeit at a sedate pace. Air travel nowadays affords no time for a gentle adjustment.

Canadian Immigration had ensured that we each had cash resources sufficient to last six months before they issued each of us with a visa. They provided accommodation in good hotels for a limited time. They helped arrange job interviews if we needed help. But they made clear our responsibilities which, if breached, would result in visa cancellation.

Fast forward 55 years and reflecting (with names suppressed): The first one got the teaching job and progressed to a successful career in senior public administration; the next one got the library job which led to a successful career as a librarian; the business

Odyssey Part I: Emigration to Canada

'wannabe' hit the jack-pot at IBM but gravitated back to academe and now contemplates retirement; the physiotherapist got the hospital job and a successful physiotherapy career but now suffers dementia; the business secretary succeeded but died far too young from cancer; the architect introduced us to Frank Lloyd Wright's masterpieces on trips around Chicago and progressed to a career highlight as Chief Town Planner for Brisbane only to die in tragic circumstances.

So, as I look out from the balcony as those ships head out on their cruises, I would do anything to turn back the clock, because that experience is unrepeatable. Though two of our group have, years later, retraced the trip on a cruise, the purposeful driving force that propelled us at that time can never be summoned up again. One can never recapture the hopes and confidence that we six had as we risked everything.

There was no turning back if we had got it wrong. An airfare back from Canada to Australia in those days cost almost a year's salary. Do you marvel at how brave we were? But then we were, in those days, a rare breed. We were **graduates** and any thoughts of needing a 'hospitality gig' as young people do these days, never entered our minds. Of course we would get professional jobs, we thought…..and we did!

In Memoriam:

Trevor (the Architect, and Sue the Business Secretary)

Vale Trevor Reddacliff 1942-2005

Trevor was from Coffs Harbour. Professionally he reached the peak of Chief Town Planner for Metropolitan Brisbane.

Odyssey Part II
from Canada on to a European Grand Tour, May - Oct 1968

Within two weeks of our arrival in Canada in February 1966, Pat was working as a physio at Toronto and I had secured a plumb job with IBM. Reflecting now, I often wonder why we left! But leave we did in May 1968 a little over two years from our arrival. Our objective was to save enough money to finance a brand new *VW Wesfalia* campervan plus living expenses for a Grand Tour of Europe which was to last six months.

We achieved that objective living an abstemious life-style in Canada. Occasionally I just had to participate in work parties such as the night the boys went on a club-crawl in Toronto. Everyone was excited that we would see Thelonious Monk live in concert. The cover charge pained me but soon after arrival the group got up to leave noticing Thelonious was 'spaced out'. We had to be frugal to achieve our aim and so, each pay day, we had a little conference and put a coloured pin in the big saving chart to record savings progress.

One lunchtime, I lined up at the bank to buy gold at $35 an ounce. The current price is about $1,800 an ounce. If only I had sunk every cent we had into gold at that price, but lunchtime had expired and so I rushed back to work!

The rigid savings regime did not preclude a lot of fun that we had living in Toronto.

Odyssey Part II: Canada and the European Grand Tour

Toronto can be cold. That's our street after a heavy snow fall when the city becomes eerily quiet as snow is a good acoustic damper. Beer doesn't need to be kept in the fridge but sometimes it can be too cold on the balcony.

We did lots of trips. One skiing trip to the Adirondacks in upper New York State sticks in my mind. As we entered the club house the live band was belting out *On Broadway*. One weekend a group of us hired a cottage in the snow and that's our water supply. Probably the best trip was the one to James Bay – a part of Hudson Bay.

Odyssey Part II: Canada and the European Grand Tour

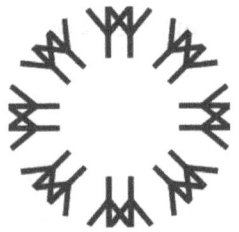
1967 was Canada's Centenary Year and we made a trip to Montreal for the major celebration festival – Expo 67. A special Vignette later in this volume describes it in detail. Montreal came at the end of a two-week holiday which swung through the New England states, Boston and Salem Mass. (site of the witch trials) and Boothbay Harbor once the pre-eminent east-coast port over New Amsterdam (New York). Thinking back, I cringe now recollecting that I subjected the aged in-laws to the back seat of a Volkswagen for this entire trip!

The swing through New England was focused on getting to Newport Road Island in time to witness first-hand the Australian Challenge for the America's Cup (12 Metre Yachts) by a boat named *Dame Pattie*.

May 1968 rolled around quickly and finally it came time to leave Toronto and North America but not before we visited New York to pick up our flight. We had found the cheapest way across the Atlantic with the Russian airline *Aeroflot*.

Aeroflot offered an added bonus of an overnight stop-off in Reykjavik Iceland. My big discovery was that Iceland should be called Greenland and Greenland should be called Iceland! From the air, the next day *en route* to Luxembourg, we could actually see the line between the sea ice and the Gulf Stream.

Odyssey Part II: Canada and the European Grand Tour   50

With much excitement we set foot on European soil in Luxembourg.

As it happened it was late afternoon on our arrival and we had to get from Luxembourg to VW's *Wesfalia Werke* in Germany. Fortunately, we had met two American lads who were also picking up a van there. We joined forces, rented a car and drove off to Germany.

We are in a German village when our travelling companions announce they are hungry and they turn to me – Herr Schmidt – to order at the little village restaurant where they speak no English. Remember this is still my first trip out of Australia. And this is the first time I had lobbed in a country where English was not the first language. I surprised myself, under the stimulus of hunger, with the amount of High School German that came flooding back!

And this is what all the fuss was about. This was to be our home for the next six months as we criss-crossed Europe. This photo is from a camping ground overlooking Vienna.

After a two-day shake-down we were more than ready for the road.

Being neophyte travellers we had not done the preparation that experience travellers would have done, though we had researched Neuschwanstein Castle and of course Venice. Another reason for heading south was that, being early Spring, south would be the direction to go. On a six-month trip, further planning could be done on-the-go, so away we went.

A big bonus was that we chose as our road south the Romantische Strasse which took us to Rothenburg and Oberammergau - Passion Play town.

Through Munich, we were heading for Garmisch-Patenkirchen where we would find Germany's highest mountain the Zugspitze and, of course Neuschwanstein Castle which Walt Disney had replicated in Disneyland L.A.

I remember the roar of jet engines as a plane took off from Garmisch below and seemed only just to clear the Zugspitze.

That's Neuschwanstein in winter.

Next we headed to Austria, in particular Salzburg and then Vienna. I knew that Mozart was buried in Salzburg and, though a pauper's grave, it was lovingly attended and smothered in colourful hydrangeas. Beethoven, on the other hand, died a success in his lifetime and has an impressive grave in Vienna.

You can tell our research was improving on-the-go because I had read of the limestone caves of Postojna not far from Ljubljana in Slovenia which was our next destination. We arrived in a German vehicle to a carousing club-house scene which cooled markedly on our arrival as they seemed unsure about us. Next day we did a caves tour akin to Jenolan Caves back home but with a dedicated guide who spoke only German – again, I rediscovered enough to get by.

Trieste on the Dalmatian Coast of Italy was next and I remember being puzzled sensing something at the famous Palace on the coastline. I was later to discover some of the history. Used as an Officers Club by the Nazis, it was the site of a Nazi massacre in 1944.

1968 was a tumultuous year. Already, when heading into Southern Germany, we had bypassed the 'Prague Spring' unrest in Czechoslovakia which had been launched on my Birthday 5th Jan 1968. It was brutally snuffed out on 21st August by an invasion of Soviet troops. On subsequent trips into this region we never missed the highlights of Prague and Chesky Krumlov but this time we missed.

Furthermore, on entering Trieste nowadays, we would first turn left for the 50 mile drive to the magnificent Roman amphitheater in Pula on the Croatian coast before a right turn to head into Italy.

It's hard to admit, but most Aussies of my era made judgements about places like Italy and Greece from the post-war immigrants we had seen in Australia not realizing that this is a poor yardstick measure of their home countries. *En route* to our next destination of Venice, the days we spent in Florence reset my erroneous preconceived view of Italy. We loved Florence as everybody does.

Venice was next. A relative in the plumbing business had disparaged Venice with its 'filthy water' as his lasting impression of his visit. Sad, and I say no more – Venice the incomparable! Ever since St Marco, the stamping ground of Claudio Monteverdi, had been my absolute favourite until years later discovering Hagia Sophia in Istanbul which now sadly has be reclaimed as a Mosque.

Rome, the Eternal City, was next but to get there we travelled along spectacular freeways through the mountainous spine of the Italian 'boot'. Not only did one appreciate the difficulties these mountains had posed in the wartime campaigns, but also one gained respect for Italian engineers and road builders. Not for the first time, the obvious lies of Australian politicians were exposed for excusing our poor roads due to the 'special difficulties' faced by roadbuilders. More and more it became obvious that there are few countries with an easier road building challenge than Australia!

One of my first LPs *An Italian Holiday* introduced me to the music of Sorrento and Salerno and now we find ourselves there after driving south from Rome.

Odyssey Part II: Canada and the European Grand Tour

I cannot stress enough the importance of negotiating this magnificent road starting from Salerno towards Amalfi, Positano, Ravello, Sorrento and finally Pompeii. Quoting the expert advice: "Rent your own set of wheels though it is not always a good idea what with the devilish curves in the road that snakes along the coast". And here we are in a VW van on a road more suited to baby Fiats or Vespas! And there is also the challenge of the big tourist busses coming at you leaving you little passing room. I have driven it twice but always from Salerno towards Naples and that's because, European left-hand-drive puts you on the inside lane rather than the outside lane hanging over the edge if you had driven it from Naples.

I wax lyrical about this drive because it truly is one major highlight of six months in Europe.

Pompeii is a must on anyone's list. In a rather conspicuous campervan, this visit was spoiled by the need to keep rushing back to the carpark lest the wheels be taken from the vehicle. At least, that's the advice that fellow travellers had given us. Years later, without those concerns, I was able to enjoy a less stressful visit.

Not to be delayed in Naples, we were heading to the French Riviera. Experienced travellers would ensure they would take in the towns of Cinque Terre before leaving Italy. Our on-the-go research overlooked all of this in a headlong rush to get to the south of France.

We found Cannes and Nice – playgrounds for the rich and famous - to be not Campervan friendly! As Australians, we looked for a van spot overlooking the Mediterranean but the best we could find was set well back close to, and on the wrong side of, a railway line! We should not have been surprised considering land values in that region!

As a result, we moved through the coastal region of the south of France quite quickly but not before taking a side trip into the walled Roman city of Carcassonne – a very special place.

We entered Spain through the Pyrenees Mountains in the border state of Andorra. It was a spectacular drive up above the cloud line in what the South Americans of the Andes region call a 'cloud forest'. Clearly the Pyrenees have constituted a formidable barrier to intruders in either direction. We were pressing onto Barcelona as our target.

Odyssey Part II: Canada and the European Grand Tour

We visited and ascended one of the towers 86 years after construction began in 1882. The construction continues now 139 years into the project which is said to be taking longer than the Pyramids of Giza. Originally a Cathedral, after a Pope's visit, it is now a Basilica.

The incomparable architect Gaudi is buried in the crypt. The Basilica towers to a height of 170 m which is higher than every Cathedral in Europe.

Spanish place-names such as Valencia, Granada and Madrid conjure up exotic images of Flamingo dancers, so we did take in one such performance. However, I would have to say that a Tango performance in Bueno Aires years later outclassed anything of that genre that we had seen before or since by a massive margin.

Our on-the-go-research was dramatically exposed for its inadequacies on arrival at a camping ground in Granada. An excited English gentleman engaged me in conversation interested that an Australian had come so far to experience the Alhambra. Nonplussed, I remembered the name only from my youth as a second-rate movie cinema in suburban Brisbane. I wisely decided not to share this with him. He told me he had come  all the way from England to Grenada just to visit the Alhambra.

Years later Ann and I, by then well and truly aware of the significance of the Alhambra, were fortunate enough to secure a top class room **within** the Alhambra itself which guaranteed first access in the morning to the complex. It was wonderful until it came time to pay the bill which literally included an extra zero in the price i.e. ten times what we were expecting. Management relented blaming the error in the original quote on a receptionist's error on his first day on the job. Really, we should have guessed that the price quoted was a bit too good by the look of our well-heeled fellow guests.

The trip up from the coast to Madrid surprised me in that Spain is really mountainous and "Spain is mainly on the (high) Plain".

By now we had been on the road for over a month. It was the 5th June and suddenly our car-radio program was broken into by very somber, mournful music. In the announcement to follow "Roberto" was all I needed to decipher that Robert Kennedy had been assassinated! As I said earlier, 1968 was a horrendous year. Martin Luther King had been assassinated on April 4th.

We continued onto to France and the highlights of the Chateau of the Loire Valley and the magnificent Tours Cathedral as we approached Paris. It was early June and **"the Blois de Bolonia is full"** was a phrase fellow travellers had advised us to use as we had chosen to set up directly under the Eiffel Tower! There we could also use the toilet facilities provided for tourists as our bathroom. Each day the gendarmes stopped by but our magic phase continued to work a treat for a whole week! It was always easy to find our way back after excursions to places such as Versailles – just zero-in on the Tower. And...what better address in Paris?

In addition to the obvious attractions such as the Louvre and Notre Dame Cathedral, we found what is described as "a gem in Gothic style" Sainte-Chapelle – the private chapel of Kings and Queens of France.

We were headed towards Calais for the crossing to Dover but, nearing evening, we decided to overnight on the coastal town of Dieppe south of Calais. Another embarrassment for our on-the-go-research was our total lack of knowledge of the significance of Dieppe. We encountered lots of somber Canadians there. On enquiry, we learned of the horrendous Canadian war losses there.

We were in a hurry to get to England as we had pre-arranged Wimbledon and Lords Cricket Ground tickets. I will never forget the spectacular approach to England framed by the white cliffs of Dover. These were the days, prior to mass tourism, when Customs officials tended to be more friendly and interested in a young couple from Australia with a few interesting stamps in their passports. It was a relief not to have to fall back on my feeble German and to actually feel the real warmth of the welcome.

The young people of Australia today seem fixated on New York and everything American whereas for our generation a trip to London and England was practically a rite of passage. In the words of Samuel Johnson (1750): *"When a man is tired of London, he is tired of life for there is in London all that life can afford".* I like that other quotable quote of his too: *"The true measure of a man is how he treats someone who can do him absolutely no good".*

Crystal Palace camping ground was our base in London and I will mention just two of the countless attractions that we were seeing for the first time: Westminster Abbey and the British Museum.

Odyssey Part II: Canada and the European Grand Tour 61

We also had a base with Pat's Aunts in a lovely thatched cottage rather like this one in the Cotswolds village of Kingham.

From our base in Kingham in the Cotswolds, we would catch the 10 am 'gentleman's special' from Oxford to London - passengers looking like brokers in their bowler hats.

The qualifying field for the 1968 Men's Wimbledon was crowded to almost half with Australians! And we were good at Cricket too. The Lords test clashed with Wimbledon so we shuttled between the two events.

We spent more than a month travelling around the U.K. One trip to Wales took us to Carnarvon where we saw the preparations for the investiture of the young Charles, Prince of Wales.

We had a truly wonderful trip to Scotland. A highlight was the

crossing by ferry that would take us in our van to the Isle of Skye. I was a bit miffed missing the ferry by just a few minutes which forced us to wait for its return. As it headed west into the sunset over that waters of Mallaig a piper piped *"Over the seas to Skye"*. Even now 53 years later, I can still hear it. It was perfect. I am so glad we missed that ferry.

By mid-July it was time for a foray back into the Continent and our focus was on Scandinavia. First stop Copenhagen and the truly wonderful shops for table ware – the name *Illums Bolighus* stays with me as it was so impressive as also were the prices. I recall the Danish Resistance Museum and the beret knitted with RAF coloured circles on the crown to assist RAF Pilots on air-drops. Stockholm was interesting as the whole country of Sweden had recently changed from right-hand drive to left-hand drive and, by their driving, I think they were still getting used to it.

Norway was the star as we drove into fjord land on the west coast. In Bergen, a South Australian visitor approached me as he had recently arrived from Newcastle on the car ferry with his new Mercedes and large caravan in tow. He had ordered it from home, picked it up in Newcastle and crossed to Bergen. He was asking my advice about how to get out of Bergen. He had spent the previous day trying in vain. I had to break it to him that even our VW van was too large for Norwegian fjord country roads carved into the terrain.

I used to say Norway was the most beautiful country on planet Earth but then there are contenders such as the Greek Islands. Nowadays, I have several 'most beautiful' in various categories.

Maybe on all great trips, on all great holidays, you get this feeling that you don't want it to end. And now we had been on the road nearly five months and money was vaporizing in Scandinavia fast. It was time to go back to the U.K. and plot a bold move.

We would drive back home all the way to India across the Asian Highway. We got the bright idea that Geoff and Judy, who had been at our table on the *Oronsay* 30 months earlier, might be interested too. We contacted them and they were interested!

But there was some organizing to do. I tried to get insurance on the van. Though the Auto Assoc was not interested, I reckoned that Lloyds of London surely would do it. Yes, they would but the cost of premiums through to India was equal to twice the value of the vehicle. Now maybe there was a message in that! We, therefore, left uninsured. One fantastic stroke of luck was that I secured the Owners Cabin on a Shipping Corporation of India cargo ship from Bombay to Sydney synchronized with expected arrival in India.

These were the busy preparations we made in London. Meeting up with Geoff and Judy we would be a party of four and would need extra camping equipment. Knowing the challenge ahead, there were jerry cans for fuel to buy. We prepared well, but our research was still of the 'on-the-go' variety. We embarked with the confidence of youth…or was it the over-confidence of youth?

The trip from London through Europe left little time for sightseeing though we did sweep through Paris. I still remember the autumn leaves everywhere and a pang of nostalgia as we left the city.

Our Grand tour had some serious omissions amongst them Switzerland as we had been tracing a big circle leaving gaps in the centre. So before leaving Europe, we took time to visit Swiss highlights.

Proceeding further I well remember, as I drove along the coast of Greece, looking out and spotting Greek Islands. I remember the 'light-bulb moment' realizing that this must be what all the fuss is about. And the pang of regret that pre-conceived ideas about Italy and Greece had been just so wrong and now there was the cost of missing out. The preconceived ideas about Italy had been rectified by our visit there but, unfortunately, there was now no time to fix the cost of missing the Greece islands. I resolved to return!

We crossed by ferry to Istanbul, skirted the Black Sea coast and reached the closed border with mountainous Georgia. Further on we passed Mt Ararat (of Noah's Ark fame) and proceeded into Iran fairly uneventfully until the story picks up in *Odyssey Part III* of this volume.

"Regrets, I had a few, too few to mention….." (Frank Sinatra) Our campervan lifestyle was centered around self-sufficiency needing a 'pit-stop' only rarely in the house of a distant friend/relative or, on one occasion, of a generous complete stranger in Germany. European camping grounds are excellent – showers are great and we did our own washing. So no regrets there.

When it came to meals, again we were self-sufficient as the campervan had an adequate inbuilt refrigerator, stove and sink. And therein lies my only real regret. Imagine, for instance, touring Italy and not eating local!

Europe on Ten Dollars a Day was a popular guide book at the time and we were getting a highly favourable exchange rate of four German marks for every dollar. However, as we had a large (by European standards) vehicle and petrol prices in Europe were high, we had actually budgeted on Europe-on-twenty-dollars-a-day which was actually quite a lot of money in those days. And we were able to keep to the budget by occasionally choosing our own spot for over-nighting. Memorable was the spot we chose at the top of the **Rest and Be Thankful Pass** in Scotland where there were no camping fees and a splash in a cold mountain stream in lieu of a warm shower. And there was that free spot **directly under the Eiffel Tower** described earlier. Nowadays, you would be moved on!

The opportunity cost of over six months of zero income was the real cost. But if you don't do something like this in your twenties, when would you do it? When would be a better time?

Odyssey Part II: Canada and the European Grand Tour

Childhood and two cameos
Prisoner's Dilemma
Austerity morphs into Abundance

Childhood

Summary

Born in Kingaroy, Queensland at the height of World War II – Peanut Country – Sunday School Teacher Joh Bjelke-Peterson (with a prize book to prove it) – Big trip to Grandparents in South Australia in 1947 – 1948 moved to Hatton Vale in the Lockyer Valley – 1954 moved to Woolloongabba Brisbane - 1954 final year primary school at Junction Park school (exhibited meteoric rise in school performance) – 1954 watched the Olympic Torch Relay at Eight Mile Plains *en* route to Melbourne – St Peters College 1955-1958 – University of Queensland 1959 – 1962 – family moved to Ashgrove 1960

Childhood

Earliest Memories

This is the earliest photo I have and it must have been taken in late 1941 or early 1942 when I would have turned one year old. There is eldest sister Dorothy looking after the baby and Bro John in his sailor's suit. Apparently, quasi-military garb was popular for kids during WW II. This photograph was taken at maternal Grandparents home in Nambour Queensland and taken by my Dad who was a keen photographer.

Childhood

Perhaps my earliest memory is from 1945. We were at a beach holiday in Tewantin in Queensland when the peace from WWII was announced and the local town council decided it was worth a fireworks display. As a four year old, I didn't understand the reason, or even what people were saying, but I did pick-up on the emotional content. Everyone seemed to be so very happy.

Later on, as a five year old at school, I remember what I now know to have been Anzac Day 1946. Hand in hand, we littlies were marched down to the only assembly area we had – the seating around the empty concrete pool. I can still remember the heat radiating off the concrete. We were 'saved' by our lovely teacher who objected to us littlies being subjected to sitting in that heat. We were allowed to return to the classroom.

A year or two later, at school now, I recall lining up with a bunch of kids and we were told to run down to what was a finishing line. I got there first and was surprised to be smothered in kisses by my Mum and sundry other Mums that were there. I certainly picked-up on the emotion that day, discovering I could make people happy just by running as fast as I could!

Big lesson here is that kids may not understand what is going on but they pick up the emotional component like a sponge. But then a pet dog can do that very well too, so it's not all that surprising.

In 1947, I had my tonsils out. So that I would not be lonely, my Mum had arranged with another mother that I'd go in at the same time as another little school friend of mine who was also to be de-tonsilled. As it happened, I was very lonely after coming out of the operation. Everyone was very careful not to tell me what had happened until years later. The little school friend didn't make it. She vomited and choked during the op as she had sneaked some mulberries from one of the trees on their farm unbeknown to her parents and doctor.

I believe these early memories are memories of events. What is the nature of memory though? Are these memories of events or are they memories of the memories: memories of the many times I recounted those events?

When I think about those WWII fireworks, I seem to be in a corridor of a house with a feeling of my smallness as a four-year-old in a big corridor! As for those mothers that smothered me with kisses, I can actually remember how nice they smelled!

In what ways has the environment changed since I was a kid

In 1996, Laura Barth, Ann's lovely niece, was challenged at the Ampang International School (Kuala Lumpur) to find some oldies and ask them that question.

This is what I wrote.

Childhood

Start of the piece for Laura Barth

I was born in the country town of Kingaroy in the state of Queensland, Australia and spent most of my early childhood in a little town called Hatton Vale near Laidley.

Both Kingaroy and Laidley were several hours drive from the only big city in the area – Brisbane though it only had a population of half a million at that time. So you see I was a country kid. I would have liked to have had a bike to ride to school, but my parents gave me a horse instead. Most city kids would think it would be great to have their own horse to ride to school. I would have preferred to have had a bike in those days. The school yard at our "one-teacher-school" had a paddock – not a bike rack! All the kids rode to school on horseback. Our mothers, since they generally had four or more kids, wouldn't have had time to drive us to school, though, about once or twice a year they would, if we were too sick to ride our horses!

We lived in three different places in my first thirteen years – moving from Kingaroy to Hatton Vale (see photo) when I was seven, and from Hatton Vale to the big city of Brisbane when I was thirteen.

Since then I have lived in many places – Brisbane until I was 25, Toronto in Canada until I was 27, I spent my 28th year in Europe, 29th year back in Brisbane, 30th until 38th year in Canberra, 39th year in Waterloo (Canada), 40th through 48th year in Canberra, 49th year partly in London, 50th through 52nd year in Melbourne and my 53rd year in Coffs Harbour.[I can add to that now: After the 54th year in Coffs Harbour, the 55th and 56th year in Trolak, Perak in Malaysia, the 57th through to the 63rd year in Kuala Lumpur, Malaysia and then twelve years in Melbourne and these last five years in Sydney].

Whenever we went anywhere my Dad drove us in the car. We travelled more than most of those country kids who had not even been to Brisbane. My Dad came originally from South Australia which is about 2,000 miles away from where we lived. We had a big adventure visiting my grandparents in South Australian when I was seven. We did this trip by train. Very few of my classmates had even visited the adjoining State, let alone visit a distant place like South Australia. Practically no-one had ever been overseas! I travelled overseas from my country for the first time when I was 25 years old and that was on a big ocean liner. Air travel used to be very expensive in my youth. My first trip on a plane was when I was about 17 years old. Mostly I did short trips on my horse. Longer trips were in my Dad's car, but we often went by train when we went on holidays.

There was no TV when I was a kid. We only went to the movies about twice in my first ten years. We read books. Because I had four siblings we played lots and lots of cards. I did jigsaw puzzles. We were always going for long walks through the bush along streams and we played a lot of outdoor sport like cricket and tennis. My brother and I made a cricket pitch in the back yard, but we eagerly awaited the birth of a new baby in 1946 which we hoped would be another brother, but it was another sister…YUK. That brother we were hoping for was going to be our wicket keeper (catcher in baseball) which would have saved us a lot of chasing after the ball if the batter missed hitting it!

If it wasn't raining, we would always spend our free time outdoors. Playing cards and reading was for the wet days. Kids today don't play as much sport as we did. They seem to spend more time on TV and computers!

We ate simple meals, certainly no fast-food, pizzas or TV-dinners (there was no TV). Potatoes mashed or baked, together with peas or beans and a lamb chop would be a typical meal. We had to finish our vegetables, or we would not be allowed to have desert. My father could not stand waste, so we had to finish everything on our plate, and he would make us stay there for ages to finish what we had put

Childhood 75

on our plate. Australian meals were very dull then, unlike now when we have a bigger variety of food from all countries around the world. We are more health conscious about what we eat these days too.

I've already talked about the walking – we were always off adventuring in the woods and fields. We didn't live near the sea so I never learned to swim as a kid. When we went to Brisbane in my thirteenth year I was the only kid in class who could not swim. I used to dread the compulsory swimming periods at school. Other mean kids were always pushing me into the pool because they knew I couldn't swim. I soon got sick of that and so I just taught myself to swim. But my swimming style is awful as a result. If every swimmer had to expend as much energy as I have to do to swim, the world champion might only be able to manage 200 meters!

When we lived in the country, we drank water from a tank. There was no hot water system for showering though. We had to hand-pump the water for our own showers and it was freezing cold. We never worried at all about pollution, we were much more worried about war. I remember how happy everyone was when the Second World War finished even though I was only about four years old at the time. Soon after that though, we kids became aware of the power of the atomic bomb, and I used to worry about that a lot.

I never wanted to go to a war but I did do a stretch in the military when my country demanded it. I know a lot of kids worry about pollution and things like that today. I still think the biggest problem is learning how to live together without war. Humans have never in history been able to do that. In this year of tolerance, I think there needs to be special emphasis on learning to live together.

Polio was a big worry for me when I was a kid. It was a big relief when we heard that Dr Salk had developed a vaccine.

Most of all, I miss the fun we had as kids. It was great having three sisters a brother. We had lots of fun and my brother is still my best friend. I don't see them all as much as we did in those days, and I miss that aspect of the old days. I certainly don't miss living in the country and I don't miss my horse and all that stuff – I'd far rather live in the city and have a nice car.

I don't really think the world has progressed that much. Sometimes I think we are going backwards when I look at the problems in the Balkans. The one area of human endeavour where we have progressed is in technology. I really believe in the global village. Computers and reaching the moon are wonderful achievements but the major change I have seen in my lifetime is the jumbo-jet. Affordable air travel for the masses has made a huge difference to the world. When I first travelled to North America in 1966 the airfares were almost a year's wages – today it would be less than a week's wages, thanks to the jumbo-jet. There are many improvements in medical treatment too.

Childhood

I really haven't noticed population pressure in Australia, but I do notice it when I'm travelling abroad.

End of the piece for Laura Barth

Other early memories

1. **Australia's population is 8 million**
   We were taught that. No wonder I hadn't noticed any population pressure. Ah, but that was nearly 70 years ago and I guess it's 23 million now!

2. **"God save the King" had to change**
   Us little kids were told one day at school that the King is dead. I remember feeling funny with the words: no more God Save the King but now God Save the Queen!

3. **A guy called Ben Chifley dies**
   One day at school they were going on and on about this guy called Ben Chifley who had died. I discovered later that, no wonder, he was the Prime Minister and he had died in office!

4. **I did a nice jig-saw of the Coronation and thought, I will go there some day!**
   As an eleven year old I was mad keen on jig-saw puzzles and I had a great one depicting the Coronation of Queen Elizabeth II. I was

very impressed with all the pomp and circumstance evident in the puzzle and I thought, quietly to myself, I'll go there one day!

5. **No *Mecanno* set though**

   Some rich kid playmates of mine had *Mecanno* sets. There was no *Lego* in our day. How we envied those with *Mecanno* sets. I am still waiting for my first *Mecanno* set.

6. **"Cheaper by the Dozen"**

   The Galbraith's, disciples of Frederick Taylor, used 'scientific management' principles to manage a family of twelve kids. My parents were obviously inspired by the story which was made into a film and my Dad frequently used this phrase in a jocular fashion. I wonder now, thinking about what meal times would have been like - 'feeding time at the zoo', whether it would have been much of a joke. I remember too how we were 'farmed out' for school holidays: boys to Nambour, girls to Bundaberg. But for us, our childhood was a ball. Parents in our day were not helicopter parents, perforce. We showed up at meal times, and the rest of the time we roamed and played. On wet days, we played cards or board games.

   When, one-by-one my older siblings went off to boarding school, I could sense the end of an era and I remember being unhappy about that.

Two Cameos from Childhood
Prisoner's Dilemma

The tuck shop beckons, but as usual we don't have any money! I'm about eleven years old and I share this frustration with sisters Mary just ten years old and Lois who is seven. We are staying with Grandparents as Mum and Dad are away travelling.

Many years later I came across the Malay-English (Manglish) expression that perfectly encapsulates our frustration: "What to do, lah?" In an early flash of entrepreneurial spirit I hatch a plan: "If we walk to and from school instead of catching the bus we will have one and six pence (one shilling and six pence) to spend in the tuck shop and that's six pence each!" Brilliant. I might have asked one penny 'commission' for the idea and left each sister with five pence to spend but I am generous in freely offering this plan.

The 'entrepreneur' still has to 'sell' his plan. Sisters are squirming: "What will grandparents think?" "Simple", I say, "We don't tell them!" The lure of the tuck-shop is strong and eventually, sisters 'come around'.

We put the plan into action and enjoy the delights of hot pies and lollies for about a week! And then all hell breaks loose. The driver of the private bus company, showing exemplary concern for the safety of the three little kids who have chosen to walk to and from school, dobs us in to the grandparents. Could the loss of revenue have been a factor in his decision, I wonder?

It is the weekend and the grandparents have dedicated two full days to getting to the bottom of this iniquity. We face a version of the Prisoner's Dilemma. We are accused and then held in separate rooms and encouraged to 'confess'. Co-operative silence between each of the 'players' will achieve our optimal outcome: the least-worst outcome. However, exoneration for the first 'prisoner' to break silence and betray the others is the powerful force that defines the Dilemma.

You guessed it, the sisters dob me in: "Peter made me do it!" So we move to the punishment phase but, In a variation of the Dilemma, even the betrayers continue to be held in solitary. It is turning into a horror weekend, and, for the life of me I can't see what I have done wrong. We earned those lollies by foregoing the comfort of the bus.

Finally on the Sunday, Grandfather's brother arrives from the 'enlightened' town of Beenleigh, Queensland. He is aghast at the goings-on and manages to secure our release.

To this day, I maintain that we did no wrong.

Childhood

Austerity morphs into Abundance

"When did you first notice Self Storage facilities (Fort Knox etc) springing up like mushrooms?" my friend Peter Kavanagh asked. Their ads talk about 'de-cluttering'. Have our dwellings got smaller? Or, more likely, have we accumulated too much stuff?

Our childhood was marked by the aftermath of the great depression and WWII. Imagine clothing, cigarette, liquor, petrol and even food rationing – the mouth-watering prospect of 26 delicious kinds of sandwiches made without butter.

Parishioners with farms augmented our food and kicked in petrol coupons that helped my father, a Bishop, do his work.

Childhood 82

And I remember my uncle, a returned serviceman with a smoking habit, constrained by cigarette rations.

And my father with just one pair of black shoes kneeling at the altar with the light reflecting from the Heinz baked-bean lid that he had carefully positioned in the bottom of his shoe to cover a big hole worn through. Recalling that, I am profoundly embarrassed particularly now, looking at my own shoes - a collection worthy of a Marcos!

Rationing was gradually phased out after the war. The last rationed products were butter, ending June 1950, and tea, ending July 1950. A childhood of austerity has imperceptibly morphed into an era of abundance!

Melded Family

Family Secrets

Happy 50ᵗʰ Birthday Michael

Wishing on the same bright star

May the light shine on the ones I love

Butterfly Kisses

Another Romantic Story

The Grandchildren

- **Photo of Seattle Schmidts on Page 102**

Melded Family Summary:

	Michael Schmidt & De Arnne	Michael Spurr & Pam	Annie Schmidt & Gary	Samantha Spurr & Ben
2004	Riley 16 Aug			
2005				
2006				
2007	Jasper 7 Feb			
2008			Zander 14 Apr	
2009		Tristan 18 Apr		
2010				
2011			Libby 28 Apr	
2012		Oliver 18 Dec		
2013			Aviana 20 Mar	
2014				
2015				Anu 1 Nov
2016				
2017				
2018				
2019				
2020				Mika 29 Aug

The Melded Family

In the chapter on Childhood, I have waxed lyrical on the joys of being raised in a large family of five kids (despite being in the least-preferred position of middle sibling!) Ann too was raised in a family of five kids in the more preferred position of eldest sibling though not of the highly favoured male gender of Asian cultures!

Nowadays though, family sizes of two (or three) are *de rigueur,* a family of four kids was bestowed on us by the course of events: Ann's Michael and Samantha and my Michael and Ann-Marie. To use an overused expression, Ann and I feel blessed.

We also feel lucky that we have four wonderful young people who are a credit to themselves. Our parenting contribution is no big secret – just that we love each one of them. We are so fortunate that they get along so well. For instance, I think Annie loves Samantha as the sister she would otherwise not have had and vice versa.

In this chapter, I will spare the kids embarrassment by not divulging too many family secrets such as first meeting De Arnne in my dressing gown at home in 13 Evans Crescent as Michael explained a minor car accident he had in Sydney, obviously not his fault!

Speaking of car accidents, there is another family story that Michael Spurr might prefer that I didn't tell – the amazing story of how he managed to write off our Volvo in Evans Crescent not 100 metres from home – thereby solving a car-leasing problem for us in the process.

Family Secrets: Breaking the Lease Bubble

We should never have accepted delivery of the powder blue coloured Volvo estate. We had ordered a red one, but when we arrived to take delivery we were asked to accept the powder blue. We later discovered that, as for the biscuit coloured Mercedes, this was the least popular colour and therefore the hardest to sell at the end of a lease.

The problem was that the 'bubble payment' at the end of the lease exceeded its resale value. However, the insurance was enough to cover the bubble. If only someone would steal it! I tried parking it in the notorious Melbourne suburb of Frankston. Somebody did try but was defeated by the in-built security on the Volvo.

One afternoon, at Mt Eliza, I got a phone call about Michael Spurr's accident. Though the car had sustained severe damage in the accident, Ann and I were relieved that, though shaken-up, Michael was unharmed. It seems that he had hit a tree in our street right in front of our neighbour's house. The neighbour, a lawyer, asked what had happened (several times): "Did the car skid and did you lose control of the vehicle?" When the police arrived Michael used the magic words: "The car skidded and I lost control of the vehicle".

The insurance company phoned me with the bad news that the vehicle has sustained substantial damage and they were considering what should be done. My business friends told me to do my sums prior to the insurance company's assessment. They said that I could offer a suggestion that, if fixing it up was a few thousand cheaper than writing it off, I would pay the difference so that it could be written off since I was concerned that the chassis may have been bent. So I anxiously awaited the insurance company's assessment.

The accident was on a Friday afternoon and I took the insurance company's phone call on the Monday: "I have some bad news for you", they said. "The damage is so bad, we have decided to write it off". I was a long way away in Melbourne so they would not have heard my whoop, whoop!

Family Secrets *(continued)*

The evening of Samantha's formal was especially memorable. As I answered the doorbell, a well-coached young man won me over instantly by addressing me as "Sir" with an assurance that, "I will ensure she is home by 11 pm, Sir!" I don't know who to blame for the breach to that assurance – Samantha returned home much later.

Annie was so worried about my treatment of her boyfriends that she drew me aside just before I was to meet a special one for the first time with the plea: "Go easy on this one Dad, he's a keeper!"

Then there was the day when I counted over 40 kids in our billiard room at Evans Crescent and remarked to Ann that perhaps we should have installed an automatic pay turnstile. That was until Ann pointed out that kids making the choice to meet their friends at home is a whole lot better option than some of the other alternatives.

There is another much less publicised, but more serious family story that should be told for the profound messages in it. It seemed to me that the occasion of Michael Schmidt's 50th Birthday was the appropriate time. I sent this e-mail to Michael.

Happy 50th Birthday, Michael! (12th July, 2021)

It was about 7:30 am on Monday 12th July, 1971 and I had showered, got suited up and was having a coffee in our rented flat in 13 Tompson Street, Garran a suburb of Canberra. I was ready to drive in to The Department of Trade and Industry where I worked. I was a little over 30 years old.

Pat, your mother, called me back to the bedroom where she was resting. She thought she was experiencing some symptoms but not really the contractions of labour pain. We pondered briefly what to do, after all the previous weekend (3-4th July) we had spent most of it in Canberra Hospital only to be discharged with a diagnosis of 'false labour' and told not to worry as that is not uncommon in the case of a first born.

Together, we made what clearly was the best decision of our lives. Eschewing potential embarrassment over another 'false labour' diagnosis, we decided to get in the car and drive to the hospital. Pat got out at Admissions, while I parked the car.

By the time I had parked the car and walked back to the Admissions section, Mum was gone. Very shortly afterwards a doctor approached me and told me that she had been taken into the

The Melded Family

Operating Theatre for an emergency Caesarean Section. He then struck terror into my heart when he said: "You better brace yourself for some bad news!"

After a long ten minutes or so, the doctor came back with some details. "A baby boy has been delivered and it is good that you got here when you did because he had tangled the umbilical cord around his legs and we just got to him in time".

All new-borns are rigorously tested, and they discovered that you had your eyes a bit out of alignment but also mild spasticity. When you were quite young we endured the stress of subjecting you to eye operations. We were so worried, but the specialist corrected the alignment very well. The spasticity was an even greater worry, but you were so lucky to have a loving mother professionally trained to treat you. Together we visited the Mosman Spastic Centre in Sydney regularly and Pat treated you relentlessly with exercises between visits to Mosman.

As a Uni student, my contribution to social responsibility had been doing volunteer work on the various Spastic Centre Fund Raising Drives, so perhaps I had earned some good karma there.

You need to know that you were a fighter – you got through a few tough early years, and your Mum and I have been, and will always be, immensely proud of you and your achievements. Who could have hoped on that day in Canberra that you would take out the Washington State Seniors Skiing Championship! - so profound has been your triumph over adversity! And we love you, Michael!

Wishing on the same bright star

Years ago, when Annie, on a Rotary Exchange Scholarship in Sweden, was studying away on the other side of the world, we found comfort in the thought that we might be **wishing on the same bright star**. In the words from Linda Rondstadt's song:

> Somewhere out there beneath the pale moonlight
> Someone's thinking of me and loving me tonight
>
> Somewhere out there someone's saying a prayer
> That we'll find one another in that big somewhere out there
>
> And even though I know how very far apart we are
> It helps to think we might be **wishing on the same bright star**
>
> Somewhere out there if love can see us through
> Then we'll be together somewhere out there
> Out where dreams come true

And that brings me to the happiest of all days when, one by one, we celebrated each kid's wedding. Michael Schmidt was first, celebrated at the Lake Burley Griffin Function Centre in Canberra. Annie was next in Daylesford, Michael Spurr at Taronga Park Zoo Function Centre and Samantha in a lovely Federation House in Newtown, Sydney.

May the Light that Shines on me, Shine on the Ones I Love: Samantha and Ben's Wedding

Inevitably, for a father, it is the weddings of the daughters that tugged the hardest at the heart strings. This is what I said in my toast to the Samantha and Ben - the Bride and Bridegroom.

"Tonight, on this great occasion, we bask in the light of a full moon out here on the terrace and the words of a nursery song express exactly the way I feel:

I see the moon, the moon sees me
shining through the leaves of the old oak tree

Oh, may the light that shines on me
shine on the ones I love.

Over the mountain, over the sea,
back where my heart is longing to be

Oh, may the light that shines on me
shine on the ones I love.

"It's all about the light. In the company of architects, I, as an amateur photographer, also know that **it's all about the light**.

We all have seen how **Samantha can light up a room**.

Ben has seen darkness and he richly deserves the light to shine upon him.

I think I speak for you all when I say, raising a glass....

May the light that has shone on us, shine on the ones we love"

Postscript-1: Later, on the Wedding Night

Sam's Brother Michael and Pam had arranged for Pam's mother Helen and father Fred to baby-sit Tristan on the night of the wedding. Returning late in the evening, Michael and Pam were stunned to hear Helen comforting Tristan who had awoken with the Nursery Song: *I see the moon, the moon sees me!*

Postscript-2: Another moon story, *OLJATO*

In the years we lived above the beautiful Coffs Harbour beaches we were closely attuned to nature. We didn't need to be told about weather fronts passing through. We could hear them in the sound of the surf.

The night view from out balcony varied prodigiously with the phases of the moon. We often chose the night of the full moon to host dinner parties. It was very obvious why beach landings in wartime had to be carefully timed to the phases of the moon, as with a full moon reflecting off the water, visibility is practically as good as day light. [A group of boat people actually managed a landing in daylight at Coffs Harbour but they were badly advised – they wore black shoes and cheap suits! Nobody wears suits in Coffs Harbour!]

We loved our location, our view, with 'the moon over the water'. Navajo Indians from the magnificent Monument Valley have a word for 'moon over the water' – **OLJATO** - which we will use someday as a house name if we ever manage such a location again!

Butterfly Kisses: Annie's Wedding

Why Butterfly Kisses? It is a Bob Carlisle song which was one of the songs I suggested be played as Annie walked down the aisle. A line from the song that means a lot to me:

> "Oh, with all that I've done wrong, I must have done something right – Butterfly Kisses at Night!"

It goes on to tug at the heart strings of any father:

> "She'll change her name today, …. and I'll give her away."

Here are the rough notes of the speech I gave as Father of the Bride.

Speech Notes (verbatim)

As Gil has sung: **"You are so beautiful!"** Let me paint a picture of this remarkable young lady:

- I was there at the moment of Annie's birth to see her draw her first breath and enter the world with a big squeal!

- Bro Michael looked her over intently as she lay on Nanna's woollen patch-work rug on the day we brought her home from hospital and asked: "What's her name again, Dad?"

- Age four, on the lifts in the Ginza in Tokyo, even respectable businessmen contrived to touch her blond hair. As if a 'black cat' had crossed their path and they must do something about it.

- Aged four in the courtyard of married student accommodation at the University of Waterloo, Canada, Annie made Angel Impressions in the snow, and she still uses my photo of that as her Facebook profile.

- At four, on the skating rink in Canada when I nearly killed the red-necks that crashed into her cutting her head on the ice.

- At four, I had to sign countless release forms before the Psychology Department Crèche would take her. This crèche runs on Piaget lines, forcing children to negotiate for toys from a *finite* stock of toys. It was to be the makings of Annie. The crèche, famous enough to be beamed on Canadian national TV, features a little bit of Annie. I still have the tape!

- At six, in one of the saddest moments of my entire life, I stood on the roof of the Athens airport lighting match after match so Annie, Michael and their Mum might see me bidding them farewell as they returned to Canberra while I had to go on to Canada to complete my Master degree.

The Melded Family

- At eight, I dropped her off at Aranda Primary School to a reception committee of little girls who, every morning, waited for Annie to arrive: "What will we do now, Annie?", they would say.

- One night after her Mum had left, my cooking was now put to the test. My first effort was Spag Bol. I did not foresee the potential disaster as Annie took her plate to the lounge room. Spag Bol slipped so easily off her plate, all over the lounge room chair and onto the carpet. I cried!

- The mornings were a challenge too. My technique at hair-brushing produced many squeals and much unfavourable comment in comparison to her Mum's expert technique.

- At the end of her final year at Radford College. I had a rushed drive from Mt Eliza in Melbourne all the way to Canberra and I simply had to get there in time. I arrived in time to hear Annie's speech, as School Captain, to an audience that included the Honourable Ros Kelly, Minister of Education. Annie was very assured. I was really proud of her.

- Later, I visited Annie in Sweden in the early stages of her year as a Rotary Exchange Scholar.

- Annie is thus fortunate to have three wonderful Mums: Pat, Ann and Eva her Rotary Mum and they are all here tonight.

- When she talked on the phone from Sweden, we felt comfort in that, although we were a long way apart, we lived in the light of the same bright star!

- Never did we have a more joyous phone call than the international phone call from Sweden immediately after the announcement: **"Sid-in-ee!** as the venue for the 2000 Olympics.

- Annie has always been there for our big occasions: The first night in our new home in Evans Crescent, first day at Mt Eliza, the first week at Southern Cross University in Coffs Harbour.

These were my notes, verbatim which I have kept to this day – because it really is a super special occasion. On the night, seeing Geoff and Judy there, I made mention of the fact that none of this would even have existed if things had not worked out right back there in Afghanistan and I acknowledged what Geoff and Judy had done to get me out of that hell hole.

I was determined not to lose it. Annie had been so composed in front of the whole School and the Minister of Education (at her graduation) and I could do it too. I was not able to touch on all these points and, though I was choosing carefully, I was to dissolve into tears near the end. Annie guided me back from the rostrum safely to my seat! I just hoped people could see what a remarkable daughter she is.

Another Romantic Story

Why should the kids have all the fun! Ann and I have had a bit of romance of our own.

We met in March 1984, and I remember a strange feeling came over me on first sight. As I looked into Ann's face, I had an eerie feeling. I felt I had sensed the future. This lady will be significant, I thought. Is this what they mean about love at first sight? My glimpse of the future turned out to be accurate.

As our years together chalked up ten, even eleven years and more, we sometimes pondered was sort of an example our non-marriage was setting for the children. It wasn't for not wanting marriage, but it was probably because both of us had been married in the past. However, somehow or another we hadn't ever gone through the formalities together.

This started to pose problems in 1996 when I accepted a posting in Muslim Malaysia. The authorities asked for our marriage certificate. For several years, I was able to deflect these demands with a story claiming that we held everything in storage in Coffs Harbour. It was amazing how long this story sufficed given that, by year 2000, we had had at least six trips back home.

The Malaysian Immigration authorities were becoming more and more insistent and so we contacted Ann's friend Bill Farmer who was the Australian High Commissioner in Kuala Lumpur. He wrote a nice letter indicating that, under Australian law, Ann and I were 'married' in 'common law'. It was nice of him to do that even though, perhaps, given his own wife's status as an Anglican minister, he may have felt that it was time that Ann and Peter were 'churched'. This letter bought more time for us as we wanted our commitment to each other not to be forced.

The proposal

In those days we travelled through Asia a lot and in 2003 we were planning a trip to India. Thinking ahead, I saw my chance as we would be visiting the Taj Mahal in Agra. In advance, I visited a jeweller in KL, unbeknownst to Ann, and carefully secreted the item in my luggage. On the day of the Taj Mahal visit, I enlisted our tour guide's help as I knew there would be metal detectors on entrance to the Taj. He was wonderfully helpful as I guess everyone is a romantic at heart. He was absolutely thrilled to be part of this top-secret scheme. In local dialect, he was able to explain what was going on and why this little bag needed to bypass the metal detectors. Thus the 'ironmongery' was passed unobtrusively, Ann blissfully unaware of our plotting and scheming.

Although through security at the gate, I wasn't home and dry yet. We strolled towards the 'Princess Di Marble Bench' made famous by the photograph of the forlorn Princess Di Spencer-Windsor sitting there, **alone**! My heart goes out to anyone in that predicament; it must **not** ever be allowed to happen. Clearly this would not be the right spot, so we ambled forward for another 20 meters or so, by now enveloped by the aura of perhaps the most romantic building on planet Earth. Our travelling companion Pam was, however, proving difficult to shake off. She would be the last person with whom I would share any secret let alone this scheme, so I now had to find a way to lose her! Not far from the Taj there is a mosque, and my brainwave was to point her in that direction telling her we would join her there. To my relief, she cooperated perhaps sensing something in the tone of my voice!

I dropped to my knees hoping that here, with even the stars aligned, so to speak, Ann would say a simple "Yes". And she did.

We hear of similar exploits on the Sydney Harbour Bridge Climb, the "Marry Me" message on the MCG score board, the proposals written by skywriters, and the proposals that are made on hot air balloon rides over Melbourne. But I like to think you can't beat the Taj Mahal! By the way, I have read that it can get a bit uncomfortable on a hot-air balloon ride, when the answer is "No"

The Wedding: October 2003
Next step: Wedding plans. Our deepest regret is that it was not possible to fly back home and make it the family occasion it should have been. Nor would the kids have been able to travel to Malaysia in time. However, we were planning a full family reunion in Malaysia for Christmas 2003 when we could celebrate together. So, for both the wedding and the family reunion in the New Year we chose Berjaya Vacation Club in Langkawi which was one of our favourite holiday 'get-aways'.

I phoned Berjaya for their Wedding Package. I must say they turned it on for us. We had one of those cabins over the water. They arranged the celebrant, the car, the witnesses, the bouquet – in fact everything at a beach resort location much favoured by young couples. One amusing note came from the Registry Office official who was the celebrant. Noticing that we were both divorced, he gave us a gentle lecture about getting it right this time!

When we returned to the cabin the Berjaya staff had set up the cabin with champagne and a lovely wedding cake.

The Grandchildren

Our return to Australia was in an Olympic Year – 2004 and our 'Eldest Grandchild', as we call Riley, was born just a few weeks after we arrived back in Melbourne.

That began a run of five grandsons: Riley, Zander, Jasper, Tristan and Oliver. On a rare occasion in 2016, we were all together in Sydney.

Travelling in South America in 2010, Ann and I often saw great stuff we could have bought for young girls but we had no grand-daughters to spoil!

However, we soon enjoyed a run of four granddaughters: Sisters Libby and Aviana with Anu and here Anu's sister Mika -our fourth granddaughter.

And the photos...

This is a very recent photo of the Seattle Schmidts on a recent Thanksgiving trip.

Michael and Pam Spurr Tristan and Oliver, Snowy Mountains hike; Sam runs an art class for Anu.

Celebrations with Grand-children at Rascal's Lodge, Jindabyne.

The Melded Family 103

On the hike, when Ann slipped off the track, Anu offers help! Anu loves her Grammy!

Libby and Anu are special friends.

Daddies love their daughters especially when the daughters are as special as Annie and Samantha.

The Melded Family 104

Not forgetting.....

The following tabulation, I'm sure should reassure grandchildren that Birthdays will not be overlooked.

Jan	Feb	Mar	Apr	May	Jun
5 GrandPa	7 Jasper	20 Avi	14 Zander 18 Tristan 28 Libby		
Jul	**Aug**	**Sep**	**Oct**	**Nov**	**Dec**
26 Grammy	16 Riley 29 Mika			1 Anu	18 Oliver

Oh, and I just like this photo! (exhausted, at the pool)

Jobs

That's me in the office of Holmes Institute, York Street, Sydney – Australia's largest Graduate School of Business - still going strong (?) in a career of 59 years longevity that began in 1963.

From the screens on my desk, it is obvious that a lot of my work can be ZOOMED. While some folks enthusiastically adopted WFH, I merely tolerated it. Strangely I never felt better than I did that first Monday morning after lockdown on a wet and windy drive across the Harbour Bridge. Seems I'm a creature of habit.

The Jobs

In Summary:

This chronicle may help in deciphering the narrative to follow.

1963-65	3	Teacher	St Paul's Grammar School Brisbane	
1966-68	2.5	Systems Analyst	IBM, Toronto Bongard Leslie Strockbrokers	
1969	1	Supply Teacher	Cab Driver, Brisbane and Nashville High School	
1970-71	2	Public Servant	Dept of Trade and Industry Dept of (Defence) Supply Canberra	
1972-90	19	Senior Lecturer	Canberra CAE University of Canberra	
		U Waterloo	1979 and 1981 Sabbatical	
		Consultant	Glass Containers Sydney Commonwealth Secretariat London INTAN Malaysia Hong Kong Civil Service Many Aust Government Departments	
1991-92	2	Director	Aust Management College Mt Eliza	
1993	1	Consultant	Melbourne/Canberra	
1994-95	2	S/Lecturer	Southern Cross U, Coffs Harbour	
1996-99	4	Dean HOS	Aust Consortium of HE in Malaysia MARA Malaysia	
2000	1	Director	Multi-Media University Malaysia	
2001-03	3	Director	Monash University Malaysia	
2004-06	3	Assoc Prof	James Cook University (Mlb/Syd)	
2007-12 May2012 2012-21	5 10	Assoc Prof Professor Professor	Holmes Institute Melbourne University Utara Malaysia Holmes Institute Sydney Dean (Academic) and Chair Academic Board and Member Governing Council	

The Jobs

I confess that I am a little proud of the 59 years 'not out' so to speak. There was a time when the family was urging me to retire. Nowadays, they are urging me *not* to retire! There is a view that time spent in "God's Waiting Room" might even advance you in the queue!

Right from the outset, I want to say that the only purpose in this chapter is to share some verities and very hard lessons learned which could potentially help others on their career journey.

I'm the exception amongst my siblings and even the extended family of my generation. I did not go to work for a single employer for life (such as the Department of Education). I took the less certain pathway of applying for jobs that I hoped I might get but laying myself open to the risk of painful rejection and periods 'between jobs'. Self-confidence was essential as well as resilience in adversity.

Holiday Jobs

I'd like to start with the holiday jobs. We baby-boomers come from the 'age of austerity' (see **Childhood** cameo). We endured war-rationing extending into the 1950s. Ours was a large, happy, single-income family but we had very little money being sustained by a meagre churchman's salary and charitable donations. How I would have liked a *MECANNO* set which many of my school friends had. I have heard that showering children with the good things of life might undermine their motivation; we experienced the reverse of that and, believe me, at an early age I resolved to do something about it. I guess you'd call that motivation. Finding jobs was part of the answer.

The Jobs

My blood boils when the younger generation say that we, the baby-boomers, had it easy. I even had to buy my very first tennis racket myself – a Pancho Gonzales endorsed wooden model – *via time-payment*. The money came from holiday jobs as a teenager.

My sister Mary and I worked at Woolworths at Christmas time and on Saturday mornings. My father ensured that we were properly mentored by the middle-aged lady that recruited high school kids. Woolworths took their duty of care of impressionable teenagers seriously and my dad often consulted with the Woolworths lady. I was allocated the cigarette counter at the Woolloongabba store, and I remember being astounded by the takings of £200 ($400) on a typical Saturday morning in 1957. They were impressed enough with me to suggest that I take up an internal tenure track to the management level. Perhaps I should have taken up that offer!

On Saturday nights I worked inserting the pre-printed colour comic supplement into the *Sunday Mail* as the papers came off the press. We worked amongst the very noisy printing machines and, by then of an age permitted to drive my Dad's car, I needed to watch the dash board lights when starting it at 3:00 am after work since I could not hear the motor tick over. I met the chief clarinettist of the Queensland Symphony Orchestra in that job. He must have needed extra cash. Subsequently, I saw him perform Weber's famous Clarinet Concerto with the Orchestra in the Brisbane City Hall.

'Facing-up' Christmas mail - a process that preceded the work of the expert mail sorters - was a job I took every December. It was easy, we just had to arrange masses of letters and cards disgorged from mail bags to arrange them all the same way for the sorters. We started at 11:00 pm and had usually finished by about 2:00 am when we could catch some shut-eye sprawled out on the mail bags before knocking-off at 7:00 am. If we had been partying in the evening prior to work, our mates would 'cover' for us allowing us more recovery time spreadeagled on the bags in a dark corner somewhere.

But my best holiday job was as an usher at the cricket Test Matches at the 'Gabba'. It was a great job because I would have wanted to be there anyway and this way I even got paid as well. One such match was the famous 'Tied Test' which I had the privilege to witness with brother John and brother-in-law Stan. Subsequently, upwards of 500,000 people have made that claim but we *were* there!

In the vacation period Dec 1960-March 1961, between my second and third year as a Physics/Maths undergraduate, I was selected for an internship at Australia's Atomic Energy Commission Lucas Heights, Sydney. Sir Philip Baxter, then the Vice Chancellor of UNSW and Chair of AAEC, clearly had established a wonderful internship program. Baxter's achievements are astounding not only in persuading Prime Minister Gorton to build Australia's first nuclear power station in Jervis Bay (rescinded by his successor McMahon) but also in establishing the National Institute of Dramatic Art (NIDA).

Baxter, even while vice-Chancellor of UNSW, directed student plays. He was a truly a 'renaissance man', though vilified by anti-nuclear zealots for his work at the AAEC.

It is depressing that now, more than 60 years later, Australians are still struggling to understand and embrace the nuclear solution to zero-emission, base-load power. Baxter will be proved right. To read more of this remarkable man, consult *The Australian Dictionary of Biography* itself the product of another renaissance man, my friend Roger's father Professor Bede Nairn.

So, the research reactor at Lucas Heights was destined to be restricted to nothing more than nuclear medicine usage. Many of us have benefited from medical scans that use its isotopes. However, I sensed even then a morale problem amongst the proud scientists working there who seemed to realise that they were out of synch with prevailing Australian political attitudes – in fact, 60 years ahead of their time. As a result, I lost interest in pursuing this as a career.

The internship provided accommodation at Baxter College, UNSW and so I had to commute a long way every day by train and bus to Lucas Heights. Eventually, fellow workers offered me a spot in a house much closer in Janalli. On 1st Feb 1961, I like lots of Australians, was glued to the radio commentary of the cricket Test Match in its closing stages in Adelaide. It was time to leave work at Lucas Heights, but I remained transfixed by my portable radio on the trip home which I recall vividly to this day:

The Jobs

"A tailender, Lindsay Kline saved Australia from certain defeat in the cliff-hanging Adelaide Test against the West Indies. With his batting, he frustrated the deadly bowling attack for 100 minutes as Australia held on for a miraculous draw. Requiring 460 to win, Australia lost nine wickets for 207 with 100 minutes remaining. A defeat for Australia was a certainty but they were rescued by Ken Mackay and No.11 batsman Kline.

As wickets were tumbling, teammates Norm O'Neill and Johnny Martin took Kline to the nets to give him batting practice to boost his confidence. It seemed hopeless as he kept getting out, but Kline proved everyone wrong in a fairy-tale performance. With the gritty Mackay (62 not out) Kline added 66 heroic runs for the final heart-throbbing 100 minutes and the Test was saved. Kline had contributed a never-say-die and unbeaten 15 runs, his highest Test score". *(Wikipedia)*

The first 28 Years: Early Career

My first real job came out of the blue just after I had graduated BSc (Physics/Maths). The Headmaster of St Paul's Church of England Grammar School phoned me offering the job of Science Master teaching Mathematics and Physics to year 12 students hopeful of matriculating into Medicine or Engineering. And their parents, footing the bill for private school fees, were more than just hopeful; 'determined' might more accurately describe their attitudes.

I suspended full-time studies for my second degree (BEcon) reverting to part-time studies and a full-time job enabling me to buy

The Jobs

a brand-new car ... a white Volkswagen beetle. (I should never have sold it). The job was a heavy responsibility for a 21-year-old, and closely scrutinised! I would advise any aspirant to a career such as this, that a teacher's responsibilities in a private school are endless. I felt at times that one would have to embrace the 100%-dedication of 'holy orders' to fulfil the role completely, yet I was good at it.

Into Business

Next was my brave move of emigrating to Canada. I was looking for an opportunity 'in business' hence the choice of Toronto and not Vancouver. In the chapter *Odyssey Part I* earlier, I mentioned my big break in cracking a job at IBM as a programmer within days of arrival in Toronto. In the spirit of sharing verities with grandchildren, I must now confess to the unimaginable career error I made at IBM hoping you may learn from my mistake - in a single word, **mentoring**!

IBM subjected me to two days of intense testing before offering me the job – physical, medical, cognitive and psychological. I was comfortable with all but one of the tests – a cognitive test in the style of an IQ test. After an hour's struggle, as the bell rang to finish, I had barely completed the first page of the 20-page test. They wrapped up two days of testing with a de-briefing session. I was told I'd done very well overall and they offered further support if I had any concerns. Tentatively, I broached the topic of *that* test:
"You have done very well on that test. The idea was to smother you

with far too much work and see how you reacted. You did well by not panicking and working methodically. We like that at IBM!"

I took to programming like a duck to water making it a matter of pride to get my programs to work (sort-of) on their first test run, something almost unprecedented. One Friday afternoon, I was summoned to the office of the big boss who commended me on my work at IBM and offered me a spot as a trainee in IBM Marketing.

I squirmed as, for me, Marketing meant being a salesman! I turned him down. He was horrified and incredulous. I recall him saying: "Well, perhaps we have got you wrong! But think about it. I'll give you until Monday morning to change your mind." And on Monday morning, I again turned them down!!!

A career in Marketing at IBM in 1966 meant becoming a multi-millionaire within five years and I had turned them down. When I have sheepishly confessed this story to anyone since, they look at me as if I am making it up or, if true, then I must be mad. How can anyone make a mistake as bad as that? Simple, in a word, I had no **mentor** to set me straight.

Years later, I discovered from my work as a consultant, something about myself that I didn't know then: I am actually a natural at marketing. And that was something IBM knew about me right from the start from the intensive psychological testing. They knew more about me than I knew about myself.

Back in Australia: Canberra Public Service

Later, resuming my career after the trauma recounted in *Odyssey Part III*, I needed lots of encouragement from Geoff Washington to re-enter the workaday fray, so low was my confidence. My career mind-set had not moved and so I sought public service jobs and I was successful at two interviews: the Department of Trade and Industry in Canberra and the Bureau of Roads in Melbourne. When interviewed for the latter, unbeknownst to me, I would have been sitting no more than 20 metres from Ann who worked at the Bureau at that time. As it happened, I plumped for the Canberra job.

You might say I must be very experienced at interviews and that's true. By now, in total, I might have had hundreds. Up to this point, (I was only 28), these were still early-career interviews when I think they are buying *potential*.

My interview experience later (see *Next 31 years*, following) is that they are focused on buying a *complete match* with the job specification and have little interest in a candidate's potential.

In addition, I formed the impression that sometimes I was there at an interview only on the invitation of a head-hunter who had to dress up a short-list. Was Sydney University actually interested in me to head-up a Short-Course Summer School? Was the South Australian Government really looking for a leader of their vaunted Multi-function Polis? These are but two of many 'exotic' job interviews where I sensed no more than a window dressing exercise.

Or it could have been that, as I was trying to come out of a period 'between-jobs', they sensed the anxiety of the unemployed. It is more difficult to move from no job to a job than from job to job.

No doubt the two public service interview successes were about potential. Fortunately, they did not detect the lack of confidence that Geoff Washington had been coaching me to overcome. But I had good reason for lack of confidence at that time. I was still medicated for PTSD – *Largactil* which has a side effect of drowsiness. On the job one day at Department of Trade, the Assistant Secretary wanted to talk to me as, shock-horror, my drowsiness had been noticed! He re-assured me that: "This is not uncommon, as people get used to the altitude of Canberra!". Whew, if only he knew.

Entry in Academe 1972
Given my North American IBM experience, I sought a role in designing Australia's first degree course in Computing at the Canberra College of Advanced Education (CCAE). In successful interviews, I managed to parley an offer of a position at the top of the Senior Lecturer range above the mid-band hurdle. That, at the ripe old age of 31, was somewhat unprecedented, to say the least. All that remained was an interview with *'Slamming'* Sam Richardson. It was the day of the Munich Olympic massacre which I heard about driving to the interview. I tried an opening gambit: "Terrible news, on the radio about the massacre of the Israelis"; "With a name like *Schmidt*, I am very surprised that you would take a view like that!"

I don't remember the rest of the conversation, I was so stunned but I asked around later and was told I had done OK: "That's one of his favourite tactics. He wants to put you off and see how you react. He's especially keen to flush out any dogmatic attitudes that you might have". I guess he didn't want to hire a neo-Nazi.

CCAE morphed into the University of Canberra, and I was to remain there, complacently sitting at the top of Senior Lecturer range for the next 19 years. What had been a coup at the age of 31, became a bit of an embarrassment by the age of 50 – though the Head of School promoted me to Director, of the University's Information Technology Centre at the 16-year mark. In the corresponding period, close friend Roger Nairn launched into the promotion circuit: first Bathurst, then Newcastle and ultimately a return to Canberra in a top job at CSIRO. The big lesson here is that the 'regional round' of promotions can be effective, and Roger is a smart guy!

I was not idle in those 19 years, far from it. It was then that I discovered my flair for marketing. In parallel with my university position, P SCHMIDT & ASSOCIATES, Director (IT CENTRE) and PYRAMIDION PTY LTD were the consulting entities within which I operated. One big discovery was that, though tempted to go it alone, I realised that 'P Schmidt (University of Canberra)' gets more work and commands higher fees than just 'P Schmidt' would. As for 'P Schmidt (Director, Mt Eliza)', this is even more so.

The Jobs

Initially consulting found me, so I had much to learn and I made many mistakes along the way. Glass Container Pty Ltd approached me for a quick review of a key staff member. Like a good consultant, I was able to parley a two-week review into an eight-year consultancy that even took me back to their parent company Consumer Glass in Canada. In fact, it was I who eventually terminated the work when Ann correctly pointed out that it really was not safe to continue to drive practically every Friday from Canberra to Sydney.

Over eight years and hundreds of drives to Sydney, various schemes were suggested to me. Get a *Cessna* and fly to Hoxton Park near the plant at Penrith. It would be safer, I was told. Brother John, for instance, had a *Cessna* licence. To my credit, I had enough sense to say no. I could envisage pressure at Canberra airport at 7:30 am with a bit of fog around – big meeting in Penrith at 10:00 am - "She'll be right!" I did not want that pressure. I had a bright idea; I would ask for a company car. Company accountant was horrified: "You've been coming here for five years, and you have *not* leased a car!". Similarly, the owner of an apartment I continually rented in McMahon's Point overlooking the Harbour Bridge and Opera House, tried to sell me the two-bedroom apartment for $55,000 and I didn't know that it would be a tax write-off. That apartment would be worth in the range of $3.5-$5 million today. True, $55k was a lot of money back in 1978, but what an opportunity missed. Lousy accountant doing my tax? Yes, a book-keeper but I, again, desperately needed a good **mentor**. Ann became that mentor.

Ten years later, as a Director of Australian Management College, Mt Eliza, the CEO made the following remark: "You are *not* the smartest person in this room Peter; this is the room where all the smart people are!" What a telling riposte! He hit on a failing and made it clear to me that I was too sure of always knowing what to do, thinking myself to be the 'smartest person in the room'. This failing might have its roots in childhood in Hatton Vale (See chapter *Childhood*) and might even have been true in Canberra, but it certainly was no longer the case now. Belatedly, I had to learn to seek and take advice. If only, back in my IBM days, I had sought advice, had sought a **mentor.**

Late one Friday afternoon I was still in the office at the University of Canberra when I picked up the phone and it was a call from London. The Commonwealth Secretariat wondered whether I could come to London next week! Easy answer: Yes. This was another big lesson I learned in consulting – the power of word-of-mouth. Someone obviously, had put in a good word. I never found out who, but I would guess someone from the Foreign Affairs Department who had been a student of mine at the University of Canberra. In its Annual Report, the University loved to boast about these connections. Even my Head of School, nearing retirement, came to me for a heart-to-heart chat about how to get these sorts of jobs!

It developed into a five-year consultancy included a full-time stint as their man in the Pacific Island Commonwealth States. Based in London, I would fly out on sorties taking in Western Samoa, Tonga,

Cook Islands and parts of Fiji. Out amongst the islands meant criss-crossing the dateline and I remember complaining about having to work two Fridays in one week. "Ah, but you're going to get two Sundays soon", they said. At the end of a stint, I would dash off my report and, being computer literate, e-mail it so it would beat me back to London. They didn't like that, I was told: "Regulations allow three days on each return to regain bearings and submit reports".

For the period based in London, they paid the rent of an apartment in the incomparable Michelin three-star Nash Terraces in Regents Park. As the saying goes in London: "Don't haggle over the salary; Ask only: Who's paying the rent?". And so it was that, after six months, they informed me that I'd had time to find something (say, a one-hour commute from the West End) and so time had come to leave the Nash Terraces. Well, time had come to leave London!

The original phone call from London was typically how these consulting jobs came to me: Hong Kong Civil Service Training Centre, Malaysia's INTAN, Eli Lilly (the drug company), Snedden Hall and Gallop (solicitors) and many Australian Government Departments. I mentioned the importance of word-of-mouth. Clearly Canberra is an ideal hot-bed for that but it only works if the word-of-mouth is made up of good words; so you are only as good as your last big job.

On the up-side, the money was good and the experience was amazing. An academic in an applied field like IT or Accounting or Architecture needs to be engaged in the practice of their profession.

It's a real pity that academe does not see it that way. I mentioned that the University liked to boast about the connections I had made but took no account of this from a promotional point of view – the holy grail of 'research' being the only way up.

Throughout the years of consultancies in parallel with my academic position, I saw that promotion would depend on at least completing a higher degree. On a sabbatical at a Glass Company in Canada, I studied my Master of Management Science at the Univ of Waterloo (and later my doctorate while in Malaysia). I was nervous when *'Slamming'* Sam Richardson summoned me to discuss my sabbatical Report a lot of which I had written at the Glass Company in Sydney before even travelling to the Canadian Head Office. He informed me it was the best sabbatical report he had ever read!

My active consultancy work led to tension with the University wanting a share of the income. My promotion to Director of a newly formed Centre was to bring the work in-house. Even then there was the jealousy of one's colleagues. A best friend (?) wrote a damming letter to the Vice-Chancellor blaming me as Director of the IT Centre for "hogging all the good consulting contacts that were won". What this colleague did not understand was the ethical imperative of avoiding the abhorrent tactic used by some consultants known as "Bait, and Switch" meaning that, some hot-shot wins the contract but, on day-one of the actual job, some light-weight shows up for the job. The client thought they were getting 'X' but they got 'y'.

It was this jealously that drove me finally to seek and win a new position at Mt Eliza. Unbeknownst to me from closeted Canberra, Melbourne was in the grip of a severe recession that had also impacted Mt Eliza. So, this was a crazy-brave move in some ways.

The Next 31 Years

The second section of my career dates from my 50th year onwards. Age 50, for some, might mark a time for reflection, for looking back. For me, 50 was a breakthrough. It was time for a party too. It was a big round number Birthday Party at our 'dream' home in Canberra and I was, within two weeks, going to be leaving it. Ann would stay on to preserve continuity in Samantha and Michael's education and I would commute back from Melbourne at least once every two weeks. So, the party on 5th January 1991 was full of hope.

Annie is always there for the big occasions. She drove down with me to the Australian Management College Mt Eliza where I was to take up a coveted position as the Director of the newly formed Executive Systems Centre having survived five gruelling interview sessions in what had been a Korn-Ferry world-wide search.

So 50 for me was definitely a time for looking forward and I remember making the decision between interview 2 and interview 3 that I would not talk about past achievements anymore and focus entirely on the future of Mt Eliza and what I could do there as Director of the new Centre strongly focused on Information Technology (IT) in business.

The first era of computing in business, of which I was an early exponent, might be characterised as the era of "The International Brotherhood of Magicians" as we at IBM sometimes saw ourselves – an exclusive enclave of the initiated. Attitudes evolved as 'information technology' as we began calling it, seeped into every type of business, and could no longer be thought of as the preserve of the few initiated ones. Moreover, I was at the forefront of educating the new generation of business school graduates. I knew that the new generation had embraced IT but I also knew there was an older generation of managers who had not. Perversely, 'old-school' managers saw desk-top computers as "expensive paper-weights" - the preserve of typists. Typically, they felt that their time was more valuable, there was a 'typing pool' for that stuff!

I knew these 'old school' attitudes and practices would have to change. Like cobwebs, they had to be swept away OR those holding such attitudes would themselves be swept away. It was a belief I shared with Mt Eliza's CEO, Professor Barry Ritchie and he had secured $6m of backing from commercial backers Digital Equipment Corporation (DEC) to research and effect the necessary attitude changes. It is rare in a paid job to have an opportunity to advance a cause in which one has a passionate belief. I was so privileged.

Securing the position at Mt Eliza marked the pinnacle of functional management for me – 25 years almost to the day from my entry into the IT industry in 1966 at IBM in Canada. But I would need more than the skills of a functional manager. Beyond imparting the cognitive skills that these managers would need, there was the more intractable affective-dimension that would need to be addressed. This is the domain of change management.

With a commercial budget of $6m came the expectation of a rigorous professional approach and a successful outcome. My approach was built on a research effort undertaken within the framework of doctoral studies undertaken and supervised in trips I took to Santa Barbara in California two or three times every year.

Practicing middle and top-level managers came to Mt Eliza typically for a five-week residential professional development (PD) program. The research-based approach of the Centre was to work in parallel with the PD program. The IT attitudes and practices of these mid-career managers were tested at the start of the five weeks. Over the period of their stay, in addition to some cognitive skills-based sessions, we addressed the affective dimension by confining access to timetables, notes, messages (in fact everything) to the PC provided in their bedroom and display screens on campus. We took inspiration from the swimming school approach even using 'total immersion' as a mantra. At the end of the program, and again four weeks after their return to their working environment, those IT attitudes and skills were tested. Lasting change was evidenced in 28% of the hundreds of mid-career managers with whom we worked.

How do you measure success? Initially I was disappointed in this metric, but psychologists advised me that achieving lasting attitude change in 28% of middle-aged persons (mainly male) is remarkable.

Digital Equipment Corporation (DEC), the world's second biggest computing company at the time was facing serious challenges as was IBM the biggest for that matter. Initially DEC would have hoped for success in selling more of their minicomputers with software known as *All-in-One* to the Mt Eliza participants in the program. This was the early 1990s and I could see that it was *MS Windows* that was 'hoovering-up' business clients. DEC responded realistically making appropriate arrangements with Microsoft. **It was the eleventh hour for both DEC and IBM.** Belatedly, I remember an edict coming to us from DEC that their new focus would not be on hardware or software but, instead, on services. I don't think it was a coincidence that IBM had earlier heavily committed to re-inventing itself as a services company albeit more successfully than the belated attempt by DEC.

Imagine the consternation amongst IBM's engineers when Gerstner was recruited as IBM CEO from *Nabisco*, a biscuit maker! And worse, when he announced that IBM needed to transform itself into a services company. IBM was to become like one of the big accounting firms in the advice business. Of course, they would still make some big computers but effectively, this meant the days of what was affectionately known as 'Big Iron', were over. Gerstner was right: IBM survived but DEC didn't.

So it was that, from the age of 50, a new vista opened up for me into general management. In my three years at Mt Eliza, I was to gradually transition across 'a ceiling' into general management. All functional managers – engineers, accountants – face this ceiling and some don't want to cross it and others want to but can't. My 29th career year began that transition from 'early career'. It was, in many ways, 'the end of the beginning' and the start of the next 30+ years that some might unkindly describe as 'the beginning of the end'!

I often joke that it has been all downhill ever since. There certainly have been ups and downs since but few ups that reached the heights of that period at Mt Eliza.

There was an immediate down. Given the DEC story (above) and the state of the Victorian economy at the time, I found myself 'between-jobs', though some consulting work came my way. Drug manufacturer Eli Lilly and Shell were two of them. The former, in gratitude, presented me with two bottles of *Grange Hermitage* at the end of the contract. A NSW Premier lost his job over less than that!

1994: Back to traditional academe

After nine months of 'in betweens', I was offered a Senior Lecturer position at Southern Cross University in Coffs Harbour. Of course, in career terms, this was a considerable step backwards. Being nearly 54 at the time and advised by one of my siblings that "You'll be lucky if you ever work again!", I prudently took the job!

It was always going to be difficult for faculty in a regional university to accept appointees 'helicopter-ed in' without serving years in the promotional queue. The new Vice-Chancellor based at the main campus in Lismore, on visits to the Coffs Harbour campus, would meet with the group of newly appointed Business Faculty members in Coffs Harbour to smooth relationships with the Campus Director who was a long-standing member of the Faculty of Education.

There was another adjustment issue on the Coffs Harbour campus. The Coffs Harbour Educational Precinct was an innovative 'pilot' encompassing three traditionally separate entities: Faculties of a University, a School of Vocational Education and an Upper Secondary College. The government hoped that such a precinct would more intensively utilize plant and equipment and I was one who believed in and supported the concept.

It helped that Ann and I loved the Coffs Harbour region, so much so that, even thirty years later, we still have our holiday home there.

1996: Australian University International Students in Malaysia
Late 1995, I was offered a position in Malaysia for a consortium of eleven of Australia's best universities ACHEM (Head of School, first of Computing & Mathematics and then of Commerce). Above all else there were clear family reasons for our interest in a Malaysian position such as this. In January 1996, we arrived on site at a rural campus maintained by MARA - a qango agency for the advancement of the Malay peoples. The campus was located near Slim River, a

place of major historical significance as the site of the last stand against Japanese troops rapidly advancing on Singapore.

We still have good friends from ACHEM, Marianne Gloet and Mike Berrell and Peter Kavanagah. We always said we could write a book about ACHEM and MARA! Two astounding anecdotes stay with me, one from the end and the other from my start in the program.

The program came to a shuddering end with the Asian Financial Crisis of 1998 and we were all horrified that it was terminated very suddenly leaving students high-and-dry, so to speak. All expatriate staff were let go with minimum compensation save for a single one, and that was me! Clearly, they had faith in me because they entrusted me with the task of finding local education pathways for all students stranded short of completing their degrees. Even years later, in shopping centres and all sorts of settings, a student would recognise me and come up to me with tears of gratitude in their eyes — a sobering experience. I realised how important my work had been.

Ironically, I nearly missed out on the ACHEM appointment in the first place. MARA officials, at the time of appointing me to help those distressed students, disclosed that soon after they learned of the list of possible appointees in late 1995, the Education Attaché from the Australian High Commission in Kuala Lumpur contacted them to effectively black-ball me! Subsequently, I discovered that the Attaché was a close friend of the Coffs Harbour Campus Director! To their credit, the MARA hierarchy ignored that advice and hired me, regardless. Though, to this day, I am saddened that someone would do that. The person subsequently suffered a nervous breakdown.

Finding pathways for those students involved many high-level meetings over more than six months. Getting appointments meant that those meetings were spaced out to the extent that most afternoons were free for me to enjoy the swimming pool at our private apartment located at the site of the 1998 Commonwealth Games (for which we had ring-side seats)! However, I was restless and was wont to complain about the idle time. One afternoon at the pool, Ann and an expatriate friend had heard enough: "Why don't you resume your Doctorate studies since you keep complaining about your idle time?" Touché! And I did just that!

Multimedia University and Monash University Malaysia
While the idle afternoons provided an opportunity to get started, within six months I had accepted a full-time academic position with Malaysia's Multimedia University (owned by Malaysian Telecom). Opportunity was backed by a strong motive driving me as well. Since I had started doctoral studies in 1992 at Mt Eliza, the ten-year rule would be evoked in 2002, meaning all would be lost and a new start would be demanded. And then I discovered that Professor Barry Ritchie, former CEO of Mt Eliza who had been my boss, was supervising Southern Cross University candidates in Malaysia (on Malaysian fees which I would gladly pay). He agreed to supervise me, and recognition of prior learning was also granted.

The Jobs

In the year I was at the Multi-media University (MMU) I had an interesting task of supervising students all of whom had a period of internship in Malaysian businesses (Malaysian Telecom had obvious leverage in obtaining enough internship positions).

The prospect of returning to the Australian University curriculum was a strong incentive in my accepting the role of Director of Business Courses at Monash University Malaysia (MUM). Of all Australian university offshore campuses, MUM would be the most successful. For instance, the Pro-Vice Chancellor was able to win accreditation from the Australian Medical Association for the MUM Medical Degree, graduates being guaranteed professional AMA recognition and licenced to practice in Australia!

As for my research, I had not much more than two years to beat the curtain coming down on the ten-year rule, and I was managing a very responsible full-time job. This could not have been done without tremendous support from Ann given that I needed to work seven-day weeks for more than two years. This I did and I even enjoyed all the hard work. As a 'Group-of-Eight' university, Monash provided support for my research in the form of research assistants. And at the completion of the doctorate, Monash activated a lovely tradition of affixing a brass plate embossed "Dr Peter Schmidt" on my office door immediately after the announcement.

I remained at MUM for a further year until mid-2004 but the pull of home was strong given that we'd been abroad for nearly ten years.

I was offered a position as an Associate Professor, James Cook University (JCU) located in Melbourne with its joint venture partner Holmes Institute. I agonised over the offer as the Pro-Vice Chancellor at MUM put it to me this way: "Peter, if you were working with JCU in Australia, and you were offered the position of Director of Business Courses at Monash – a Group-of-Eight university – at its campus in Malaysia, I *know* you would take it!". Yes, but I was 63 years old, and no matter how much we had enjoyed the years in Malaysia, there were other factors to consider: the family (potential grandchildren) and a neglected Superannuation and retirement plan.

Back to Australia with JCU: International Students in Melbourne
I accepted the JCU position (and their offer to pay the relocation expenses back to Australia!). If ever I needed to see proof of why all those seven-day working weeks were necessary, it was this. There is no way I would have been recruited from abroad without a doctorate. The status of Group-of-Eight, no doubt, helped as well.

Ten years after leaving Melbourne, we were back again. Flying out from tropical Kuala Lumpur on 30th June, we arrived 1st July 2004 in freezing Melbourne. We took weeks to acclimatise.

While Melbourne was the centre of the JCU/Holmes JV, I was also entrusted by JCU to manage the academic issues at the Sydney campus. Frequent travel between the two cities was necessary.

On 30th June 2006 after three years, JCU decided to retreat back north of the Queensland border ending the highly successful JV!

Now this really looked like retirement. I was 65 and we had a large development project to manage in Coffs Harbour. Earth moving equipment and a steam roller were involved so this was much more than a handy-man effort. Together Ann and I got into it. Our kids were horrified later when they learned that Ann had been adept with a chain saw in hacking back an out-of-control tropical garden (jungle). We even hand-mixed and laid a concrete slab and tiled it!

In those few months of 2006, we were transforming 7 Sapphire Place, Sapphire. Apart from the earthworks and garden, we needed to rehabilitate the property after a dodgy tenant (see Vignette *On Remote Renting*). Various 'tradies' suggested ways in which we could make money out of all this hard work. One scheme was to get into Blueberries which were proving more profitable than bananas - Coffs Harbour's staple. Maybe, we should have taken up that idea!

In October 2006, Holmes Institute phoned offering me a six week assignment in Melbourne. I accepted: Ann would remain in Coffs Harbour, and I would commute to Melbourne. Just as the review at the Glass Company blossomed into an eight-year consultancy, the six week assignment at Holmes remains active still after 15 years.

Holmes Institute is a multi-sector RTO meaning they offer educational programs at three levels, Upper Secondary, Vocational and Higher Education (at degree level). Joint Ventures with James Cook (see above) and Newcastle Universities had enabled them, with their JV partners, to offer programs up to post-graduate level. Now, without the support of the JVs, they aspired to go it alone.

At a company retreat in Hong Kong, I made a 'pitch' advocating that Holmes could establish a Graduate School of Management starting with offering its own MBA. Dating from 1991 at Mt Eliza, I had had more than 15 years of experience in delivering MBAs. The success of Holmes Graduate School has been outstanding recording 92.7% compounded annual growth (year-on-year in its first seven years)!

My teaching areas are in Innovation & Entrepreneurship and Management. Once, in a social setting with an Australian academic, I proffered a positive generalisation about students of today. I was queried: "How long, Peter, since you have taught an Aussie student?" He was right! It is more than 25 years since I have taught an Aussie student. But I do have expertise in International Student Higher Education derived from those 25 years. In addition, I point out that I was an international student myself at University of Waterloo.

My role at Holmes increasingly became a development one, documenting each step in a formal submission to the Regulator as course accreditations and Institute re-registrations. To date, I have been primarily responsible for seven such submissions, each to a deadline, and each granted maximum period. Strangely, soon after each deadline, a trip to hospital seems to have been necessary in the aftermath of the release of the tension that had been sustaining me!

In May 2012, I was appointed full Professor at Malaysia's second largest university – University Utara Malaysia. As it happened, I never took up the position as Holmes Institute made a counter-offer. I stayed, and a move to Sydney campus became permanent in 2016.

Reflecting

Thinking back, there is no doubt that my turning down a marketing position at IBM in the mid-1960s, at a time when they had such a dominant business presence, was catastrophic. It is unimaginable that anyone could make such a mistake!

Agencies from two different governments, seeing what IBM had seen, entrusted me with high-level marketing: A SE-Asia Aus-Embassy blitz funded by *AusTrade*; Trips to Shanghai and Beijing funded by *MaTrade*.

In the 1990s in Malaysia, it was almost as if history repeated itself. Mike Berrell and I, over cold beers on hot tropical evenings, discussed starting a college for international students in Australia. We realised we had a perspective that few could match since we were so early into this field which was destined to blossom. Ann joined in our fantasies that included a mythical 'rich uncle' who would finance the venture. But we never acted. Sadly, we can name several organisations, flourishing in the international student market in Australia right now, despite having less relevant academic 'cred' and experience than we had. What we were missing, again, was the appetite for commercial 'risk-taking', for want of a better word.

Maybe I should have focused on business rather than academe. I say that because academe is held in low repute these days, and not valued as it was even in my student days. Sadly, academe itself has contributed to its own eroding reputation which, in turn, reflects on the academics within the system.

Yet, glancing through this chapter, I do have to be happy with what I managed to achieve. Recall the Orientation Day exhortation of the University of Queensland's VC: "Of you, much is expected!"
I can't help wondering how my career might have played out were it not for the severe set-back detailed in *Odyssey Part III* earlier. In that chapter, I mentioned that I would never allow myself to think that way. I would never allow an excuse such as that to let myself 'off the hook', so to speak. But now, in review, it is legitimate to ponder such a question.

The real set-back was the ten years I spent obsessed with Contract Bridge because I needed to prove something to myself. Those were the years I should have been working on my doctorate. I did get there in the end, becoming somewhat of a late-bloomer!

What I will say to those who question my continuation in work: "It has taken me a long time to get my hands on the levers and I confess that I am in no hurry to let them go!"

Vignettes

Luminaries	137
Adventures and Revisits	141
Trans-Siberian Railway	159
Travel Sickness	169
The Trip that Didn't Happen	179
EXPO67	185
My Walk in the Woods	197
America's Cup	199
Sailing the Great Lakes	219
CityCat and RiverCat	223
Brisbane: 'River City'	227
On Remote Renting	237
On Boredom	241
On Books	245
On Music	251

Luminarias of Albuquerque

A **luminaria** is a candle contained in a paper bag and placed outdoors with hundreds of others on a pathway or an abobe flat surface. They glow when the candle is lit and are a beautiful simple way to spread the light of Christmas.

The Luminarias of Albuquerque

The woman in front of me bends over to scoop the sand into a small brown paper bag. She will carefully place an elongated 'tea candle' on top of that sand in this common 'sandwich bag'. She had made a single luminaria .

She, along with countless citizens of Albuquerque, will spend the next few hours making thousands upon thousands of these luminarias. And then they will carefully light each one.

You can feel the love in these smiles. You can feel the warmth, the excitement as Albuquerque Old Town prepares for its night of the luminarias.

More than ever now in pandemic times, we need these smiles.

At last, I'm back to share in that special experience. It has taken me all of 31 years to get back here to honour a pledge I had made with myself back in 1979. I always knew I would be back, so intense was that first experience of Albuquerque's luminarias. And I have come half-way around the globe for this night – all the way from Melbourne, Australia.

Back in '79, a snowfall amongst the lights intensified the experience which has inspired family occasions ever since - the luminarias which we laid out for my father's last Christmas Eve in Brisbane. We used them to light wedding pathways too.

Luminarias of Albuquerque

There is no snow in Albuquerque tonight, but it is a nice crisp, windless evening ideal for luminarias. We're staying right in the heart of things at the Hotel Albuquerque, Old Town and we have arrived early enough to see the preparations.

We're well prepared - we even have an internet, pre-paid booking on a Luminaria Tour. Luckily we arranged this in advance, since all seven tour timeslots have long been sold out.

The sheer complexity of the tour operation astounds us. Each of the seven departure times involves a convoy of 18 busses escorted by police on motorbikes. The logistics demand that the bikes must get to the front of the convoy to stop traffic at each intersection and then, having shepherded every bus in the convoy through, must speed back to the front of the convoy in time for the next intersection - each bike lit up like a Christmas tree.

The tour visits key points in the city, none more dramatic than the municipal park where the only lights allowed are luminarias. In their authenticity and simplicity, this mass of luminarias, set out on adobe flat surfaces, define this event like no gaudy display of neon lights could ever do. And it is this authentic, simple yet powerful phenomenon that really was worth coming half-way around the world to see.

Walking back from the tour, we enjoyed the sights of the Old Town including a Manger Scene complete with live animals.

The Tradition
The tradition dates at least to early 17th century Spain. In one version, people burned cedar boughs along town paths, symbolically lighting the way to Bethlehem for Mary and Joseph. A slightly different version suggests that luminarias were intended to brighten the way for the Magi. The tradition is a feature of Christmas festivals in the American Southwest where luminarias light the way to many Christmas celebrations.

Adventures and Revisits

Ann and I are inveterate travellers; we don't do cruises, we do voyages! That's a bit like not doing tunes but doing music. Perhaps, there is value in sharing our experience. Let's start with adventures.

Adventures

By far my biggest adventure was detailed in ***Odyssey Part I*** earlier. This was no cruise; it was a risky gamble. How brave we were forgoing six weeks wages (for the duration of the **voyage to Canada**) with no sure future on arrival and limited cash reserves. If ever there is a time for such a gamble it would be when in your twenties (like we were), or in a 'gap year' (popular now). And our gamble paid off.

Just three years later, again in our twenties, we undertook another risky gamble in driving overland from Europe across Asia (**Asian Highway: London to Mumbai**) as detailed in ***Odyssey Part III*** earlier. Sadly, this was a gamble with quite a different outcome.

Ten years later, we again embarked on an overland Asia/Europe adventure, this time crossing in the reverse direction. For ten years I had wanted to re-do the Asian Highway "to prove something to myself!" However, this was absolutely forbidden by family and medicos. Furthermore, with the added responsibility for two children, Michael and Annie, it was time to be a little less risky and undertake, instead, the **world's longest train journey from Vladivostok to Berlin.** (see *Vignette: **Trans-Siberian Railway**)*

A **voyage to Antarctica** is an adventure experienced by only a privileged fraction of humankind, each landfall limited in the number permitted to go ashore at any
one time. Feeling like humans stepping on a beautiful alien planet, we were met by a delegation of penguins: "Take me to your leader", we could have said. However, there are strict rules about not approaching the penguins.

Susceptibility to sea sickness and an Argentinian ship lacking stabilizers, was a risky combination. Departure was scheduled to allow time for a formal dinner on-board as the ship steamed up the calm waters of Beagle Channel. After dinner, as the ship entered open water *en* route to the **notorious Cape Horn and Drake Passage** beyond, we
noticed that the crew had thoughtfully attached sea-sickness bags to all handrails spaced just a single pace apart! "What have I done, putting us in this predicament", was the refrain boiling through my brain as I endured an authentic panic attack. I calmed down as we experienced atypical tranquillity. The crew joked about 'Drake Lake', and I was even able to photograph reflections on the calm water.

Adventures and Places to Revisit 143

An unparalleled adventure, sailing in the light of the midnight sun!

Though fearful of a more typical return across the Passage, we were very lucky as it was calm then too.

Our trip to **Israel and Jordan** was also quite an adventure. Walking the actual Stations of the Cross and the Garden of Gethsemane evoked childhood memories of Sunday School. Also impressive is Israel's careful husbanding of every drop of water, sadly a lesson still to be learned by Australians living in a dry continent.

Jordanian highlights included floating on the Dead Sea and enjoying the therapeutic benefit of the Dead Sea mud. Now we were the ones who looked like aliens!

Visiting the ancient civilization of **Petra** in the tracks of Lawrence of Arabia …..

through the Wadi Rum and 'glamping' in the desert are the other compelling **Jordanian adventures**.

Itching to Return?

If funds and time were unlimited, there are three regions and two absolute favourites to which I would return again and again.

Firstly, South America:

Topping the South American list are: Machu Picchu (Peru); Perito Moreno Glacier (Argentina); Iguazu Falls; and Torres del Paine (Chile).

In **Melded Family** (p.101)………….

"Travelling in South America (2010), Ann and I often saw great stuff we could have bought for young girls but we had no grand-daughters to spoil!"

But we bought it anyway, and we get to give it to granddaughters now.

Adventures and Places to Revisit

The right way to approach Machu Picchu - surely one of the foremost wonders of the world - is by trekking the Inca Trail. For us, this approach was precluded by a broken wrist sustained earlier in El Calafate (details in **Travel Sickness** p. 176). Yet this was **not** going to deter us as we were particularly determined to get to Machu Picchu on this trip as, on our first trip two years earlier, travel to Machu Picchu had been foiled by a mud-slide closing access for months.

We took the special train in from Cusco and the connecting bus ride up the hairpin bends. Viewed from the bus as we approached, it is not hard to see how the complex was 'lost' being entirely covered by jungle. Another big question is: What happened to the Incas?

At **Machu Picchu**, be advised to stay at the chalet inside the gates as you will get the jump on all comers next morning since you will not need to queue as you will already be inside. Yes, though expensive, that can be offset if you remember to order the most expensive wine for dinner. (It's an all-inclusive price).

The day before the disastrous fall at our hotel in El Calafate on Lake Argentina we had cruised around the **Perito Moreno Glacier**.

Fortunately, we had had the Perito Moreno adventure to undoubtedly the most impressive glacier we had ever seen (and we have seen a few).

Spotting a mass of pink flamingos on Lake Argentina as we returned to El Calafate, I had intended to photograph them the next day but it was not to be.

Earlier, on the Brazil/Argentina border, as we walked towards the **Iguazu Falls**, I mentioned to members of our party that I had been to Niagara Falls in Canada and was not about to be impressed. A few minutes later I was literally gob-smacked!

Adventures and Places to Revisit

I read later of Elanor Roosevelt's famous exclamation **on seeing Iguazu for the first time**: "Poor Niagara!"

We stayed in the nearby hotel accessing the falls with a dedicated tourist train every morning which was smothered by butterflies following the train.

Torres del Paine was voted first by American readers of the National Geographic as 'The World's Most Beautiful National Park'.

It is fantastic,
but come ready to do the walks.

Adventures and Places to Revisit

Secondly, North America:

North America, of course, seems to have everything but I would single out the **New England states**. Cruising from New York up the East Coast to Maine and then to the Gulf of St Lawrence, the St Lawrence River and finally the St Lawrence Seaway. This extraordinary trip could take you all the way to Chicago in the mid-west *by water*. Quebec City, Montreal, and the Thousand Island Region are all accessed *en* route. (See *My Walk in the Woods*)

Thirdly, Europe: (See also *Odyssey Part II, European Grand Tour*)

Europe of course rates highly as evidenced by this short-list: Cesky Krumlov and Prague in the Czech Republic; London; Scandinavia: Helsinki and the Lofoten Islands and fjords of Norway.

Franz Ferdinand was banished to this beautiful castle in **Cesky Krumlov** because he 'married out', i.e. married a commoner. The Hapsburgs discovered something the Windsors needed many more years to discover. Franz Ferdinand couldn't keep out of politics which led to his assassination by a gunman - an act that triggered World War I. I think he should have stayed in Cesky.

We visited in both summer and winter, winter being my favourite.

Adventures and Places to Revisit

We visited the museum of Egon Schiele a famous artist who had his studio in Cesky Krumlov. He was an artist collaborator of Gustav Klimt. Here, Ann views the original of Klimt's *The Kiss* on display in Vienna. I assumed Schiele was a war casualty when I saw, at the museum, that he had died in 1918 as a young man. I discovered his wife also had died in  1918, in fact, both casualties of the Spanish Flu pandemic.

While on the subject of the Hapsburg Empire ('Danubian Empire'), the astounding Budapest Parliament House building makes any European short-list. Add the horrendous monument of the bronzed shoes of the Jews thrown into the Danube *sans* shoes.

Adventures and Places to Revisit   151

"If you are tired of **London**, you are tired of life", is the famous saying. Whereas our generation looked to London, the current generation seems firmly set on New York! Why?

Scandinavia is breathtaking. **Helsinki** is a wonderful city - the home of Sibelius. (See: ***On Boredom***)

The Norwegian **fjords and Lofoten Islands,** particularly in winter, are astoundingly beautiful.

Absolute Favourite

As for my absolute favorite of all places to revisit, I would find it hard to separate Egypt and the Greek Islands as joint favourites.

The Greek Islands

I remember, after touring Europe for the whole summer of 1968, driving out to the Asian Highway and passing along the Greek coastline around Thessaloniki in the early part of that trip. (See ***Odyssey Part III***). I looked across to the Greek islands and said "Ah!". For the first time, I understood what it was all about. But it was too late, we were committed to the Asian highway. I vowed to return, and this I did many times.

It was more than twelve years before the first opportunity to revisit the Greek Islands finally emerged in 1981. About a week before departure, Aegean Tours, our travel agent phoned to ask whether we were still going ahead with our travel plans. I thought it an odd question to ask even though there had been something about earthquakes in Athens on the news. Of course, we were going ahead with travel plans to Greece, plus a research trip to Moscow and onto Canada to complete my Master degree.

On arrival, I remember noticing the tents on the grassy strips between the carriage ways of the roads from the airport into Athens. I remember thinking that there seems to be some kind of Scout's Jamboree Event on in the city. Later that night, sleeping soundly in the hotel, I suddenly found myself on the floor – aftershocks! Aussies

Adventures and Places to Revisit

don't know much about earthquakes and why people choose to sleep in a tent outside rather than a room inside a high-rise hotel.

Notwithstanding all that, we had a wonderful time starting with a visit to a friend's house on the waterfront in **Galaxidi** and

continuing with a drive around the **Mani region** of the **Peloponnese** thus proving that there is much more to Greece than just the islands.

The Greek Traditional Settlements were our target, island-hopping between selected Greek islands. I liked the Traditional Settlement concept of immaculately restoring heritage sites and making them available for rent by foreign tourists. This was my chance to experience its realization. Back home, such sites invariably end up as museums, so I was impressed that the Greek government had devised a different plan – one that really suited us as tourists.

In my enthusiasm, I made a photographic record of the ones that we had stayed in and, on return to Australia, I was able to sell the photos to *Aegean Tours*, a large travel agency selling Greek tours to Australians. Though I didn't make much money out of it, it was such a buzz visiting any travel agent anywhere in Australia and asking for the *Aegean Tours* brochure....and admiring my own photos!

Adventures and Places to Revisit 154

Santorini is the result of the biggest volcanic eruption in known history and that accounts for its geological composition entirely of pumice stone. The authentic Traditional Settlement in Oia is a series of caves dug into the pumice stone. So immense was the eruption that there is speculation that it accounts for the lost city of Atlantis.

Blue domes with the white of the buildings reflect Greece's national colours as seen on their flag. Our most recent trip was at the start of the season at Easter – a great time for a visit to Greece.

Adventures and Places to Revisit 155

Everyone would have a favourite Greek island, perhaps Mykonos? Here I mention just two: Fiskardo on Kefalonia and Chania in Crete.

Kefalonia is of the Ionian Island group, quite different from Cycladic group.

The bus trip to Fiskardo from the port is so difficult that privacy is guaranteed, secure from all except yachties! Perhaps that is why Prince Charles and Princess Di chose Fiskardo as a honeymoon retreat anchoring the *Britannia* just offshore.

Crete not only has the beauty of the Greek Islands, but also has a wealth of history dating back 7,000 years to Minoan civilization in evidence at the palace of Knossos. We were surprised to see authentic wall tiles featuring dolphins!

The more recent history in the area around Chania is of the German paratroop invasion, the first time that such a tactic had ever been used. Allied forces included Australians and New Zealanders, fallen in the great numbers of white crosses in the Allied War Cemetery.

Adventures and Places to Revisit

German losses also were heavy. Their war cemetery, denied for over 50 years, is impressive now that it is built. Red-flowering pig-weed is used instead of white crosses creating a 'blood-on-the-battlefield' effect. I was impressed that the German government brings in rosters of high-school student groups to do the maintenance.

Egypt

One cannot fail to be impressed by Egyptian civilization dating back more than 6,000 years. The hieroglyphics they developed for documenting their civilization have left a legacy on papyrus and stone so voluminous and fascinating that many enthusiasts before us have been drawn to a lifetime of work in deciphering them. [The capability to document and record events enables history to be written. Scholars believe this to be a key building-block in developing a society which might learn from past triumphs and mistakes].

To have entered **the tomb of Tutankhamun** is an incomparable privilege save for having set foot on the continent of Antarctica. There is no doubt that both experiences are very, very special.

Adventures and Places to Revisit

Napoleon spent the night in the Great Pyramid of Cheops and would never divulge anything about the experience.

Some perspective on the engineering triumphs of the Egyptians is evidenced by the fact that humans were not able to build anything taller until Eiffel built his Tower in Paris five thousand years later in the late 1880s!

The colossus of Abu Simbel is further evidence of the engineering capabilities of the ancient Egyptians.

I like the way ancient Egyptians appreciated beautiful women in contrast with some neighbouring States obsessed with the covering-up imperative - a huge step backwards. Their appreciation found expression in Egyptian jewelry, made thousands of years ago, yet still as good as anything made today.

Trans-Siberian Railway

July 12, 1979

This was a momentous day since it was to be the first time in a little over ten years for travel abroad since that ignominious homecoming in December 1968 (see *Odyssey Part III*). Re-establishing a career, becoming parents, and building a house had been the top priorities.

We were waiting at Sydney International Airport for departure and the big flight schedule board was swamped with *'DELAYED'*. It seemed that every flight was delayed, and we had no explanation.

"(In the USA) Restaurants began marketing 'Skylab cocktails. (Drink a couple and you won't know what hit you), while beanies embroidered with bullseye were sold as a safety precaution – logic being, the US Government couldn't hit anything it aimed for!" *(Google)*

The world was waiting for Skylab to come down. It had been pushed off a course over Europe and America, but they figured there is a large area of water in the southern Indian and Pacific Oceans and, even if it hit land, there is a large area of vacant land across Western Australia - and that is just where it *did* hit. Suddenly the flight schedule board livened up and we were off and running!

Sundowners was a very popular adventure tour company specialising in *In-Tourist* trips through the Soviet Union. With the kids, Michael (8) and Annie (4) on their very first trip abroad, we took a swing through Asia before joining the group in Yokohama (after enjoying Japan for the first time). By ship, we crossed the Sea of Japan to disembark at Nakhodka close to Vladivostok, the east-most port of the Soviet Union (as it was in those days). **See map page 34.**

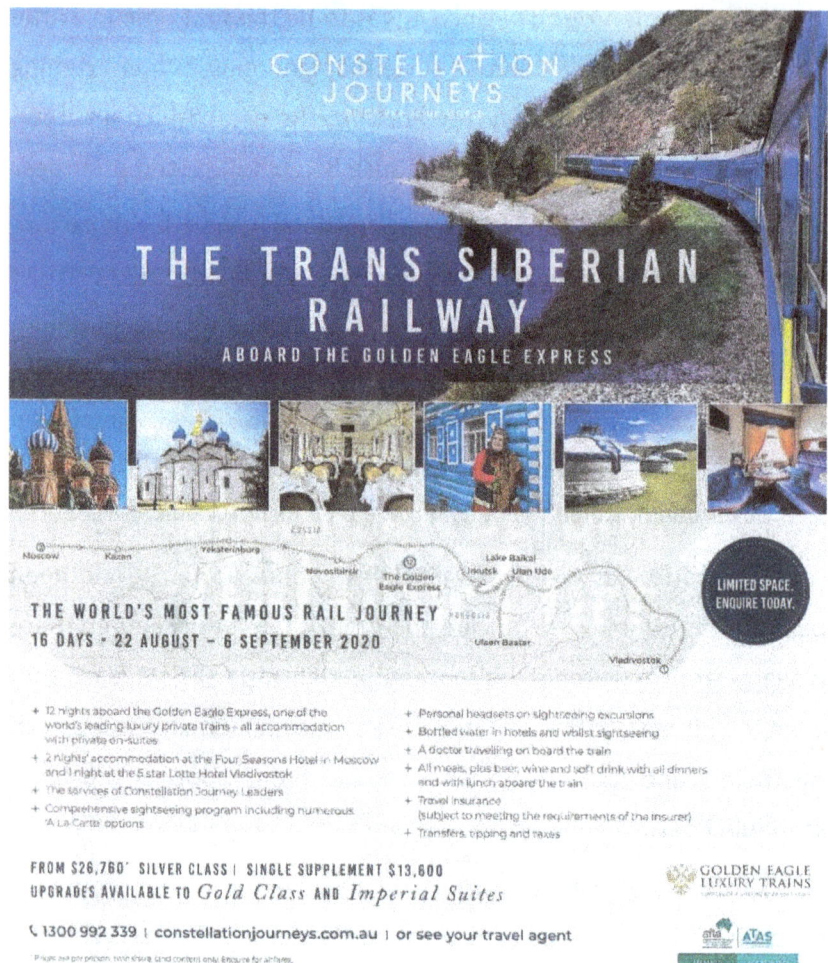

Trans-Siberian Railway

We had passed very close to North Korea and now, on the train, we were entering the highly disputed China/USSR border area. The reality of this came to us very suddenly soon after boarding the train when we saw a small missile shoot at very high speed from behind the camouflage of a haystack not far from our train! Our *In-Tourist* Guide reassured us that this was 'normal' and we were not to worry!

Our family unit filled a four-berth austere sleeper which opened onto a corridor where Michael and Annie could roam, and I could photograph the passing scene. It was a big adventure. Whenever the train stopped the kids were very popular with the locals. Sting got it right when he sang: "Russians love their children, too".

We developed an empathy for the locals and their dismal plight as it was obvious that 'the system' was not working for them. [Several years later, on a train from Athens to Moscow, I chose to travel 'first-class' and found myself alone in the entire carriage. At each stop, poor peasants - some mothers with young babies - on noticing the obvious space, tried to board my carriage. It was sickening to watch guards, pushing them back using rifles as battering rams! Lenin, I'm sure, would turn in his grave.]

In-Tourist, as a condition of travel, required a designated spend every day but there was little to spend it on – the fruits and treats you would expect to buy on platforms at train stops were of abysmal quality. I guess peasants had little incentive to do better but the one thing I did admire were the small vegetable plots they tended for themselves which use any available land in the train track corridor.

It was difficult to spend the allotment that we had been forced to convert into non-convertible roubles let alone the kopecks! As I imagine they say in Russia: *'Look after your kopecks and your roubles will look after themselves'*. (100 kopecks equal one rouble). In desperation, I considered mink coats only to discover that luxuries can only be bought in $US! We bought some Babushka dolls of course and I had a brainwave to invest in a chess set, but all I could get was a plastic one made in Taiwan!

An enterprising American, who happened to be in our carriage, took me aside and showed me a suitcase half full of roubles that he had been 'hoovering up' from those of us who couldn't spend them. He had a plan. This was 1979, and next year being 1980, the Olympics would be held in Russia. He would take all those roubles back home and sell them off to Americans who would travel to the Games. Well, I wonder how did that go when a few months later, the American President boycotted the Games!

Our Australian *Sundowners* group were interesting folks – we even had one elderly member of the Kidman family travelling alone. Our *In-Tourist* guide was there to keep us out of trouble helpfully warning when not to take photographs! She was very well educated and a real Anglophile who dreamt, one day, of visiting London!

Trans-Siberian Railway 163

The early section of the train trip is perhaps the best part following as it does the Amur River's Course through wooded mountains. Silver Birch were in profusion and, since living in Canada, they had become a favourite of mine. We were to see many millions more by the end of the trip until it was almost too much of a good thing.

As mentioned earlier the Amur River marks the disputed border with China, each side believing it necessary routinely to fire off warnings to the other side!

The remarkable town of Irkutsk was our first stop-over, noted for wooden hand-carved traditional houses. The stop-over included a boat trip on an even more remarkable Lake Baikal nearby.

This single lake alone contains 23% of the planet's entire water supply whereas the five Great Lakes in North America in total account for only 21%. From a surface view of these lakes, you would never guess that Baikal alone contains more than the total of all the Great Lakes. The explanation, of course, is in the depth: Baikal's Average Depth is 5,387 feet (that's more than a mile), and the Great Lakes' average is 195 feet. Baikal sits on a fissure of the earth's crust.

Back on the train the next day we settled into a routine for the four-day crossing of Siberia. I breathed a great sigh of relief that we were not doing this in the endless white snow of winter, though the endless green of the Silver Birch also became a bit monotonous.

Adding to the monotony was the flat nature of the landscape which persisted for days on end until we crossed the Urals marking the transition from Asia to Europe.

A Moscow stop-over of several days was astounding. Golden 'onion' domes and Saint Basil's on Red Square attest to its glory days. We stayed at a relic of its past – the Hotel Metropole on Red Square. The obligatory visit to the Kremlin to view the embalmed body of Vladimir Lenin was another highlight. I was asked by the guards to lower my gaze out of respect for the great man.

There were two dissonant elements, however, that could not be ignored. First, the shopping was dreadful and the second, the Russian word "Nyet!". I think it is a glass-half-empty phenomenon.

Trans-Siberian Railway 165

At a taxi stand, I asked directions from a Russian and got the expected "Nyet". Exasperated I retorted: "Nyet, nyet, nyet, why not Da!" at increasing volume. As we jumped into the taxi, I was astounded that, in embarrassment, he threw about 10 roubles to us though the open window. As we sped off, I had no time to apologize or to thank him.

Included in our itinerary was a side-trip to Leningrad (now St Petersburg). We did the trip by overnight train but with the blinds down throughout by the decree of our *In-Tourist* guide. Despite the tragic history of the barbaric siege of Leningrad, it is now the jewel in the Russian crown. The Summer Palace and the Winter Palace of the Hermitage are without parallel. The city itself has waterways and Italianate architecture inspired by the canal city of Venice.

A student group engaged with me at the Hermitage and invited me to a student party that evening. I waited at a designated intersection to be picked up and was shocked that I was bundled down on the floor of the back seat of the car and covered by a blanket. I was ushered into the apartment still under the blanket, yes, really!! They explained that the cloak-and-dagger security was necessary as the Soviets have an entrenched system of busy-bodies (usually older women) who dob-in anyone engaged in 'suspicious' behaviour – and that means anyone engaging with the dreaded foreigners! I thought back to some old movies I had seen that depicted a very similar system of old crones dobbing-in fornicators to the Catholic Priest.

It was a genuine student group anxious to engage with a Western foreigner - a fantastic evening centred around copious quantities of pepper-laced vodka. I was returned to the pick-up spot in the same manner as I had arrived. However, now the canal bridges were open, so I had to wait until early morning until they were lowered before I was able to get back to my hotel.

With the highlights of the trip behind us, *Sundowners'* focus was now on getting us to Berlin with as little fuss as possible. I do recall peering out when we stopped at Warsaw's *'Hauptbahnhof'*. The big sensation was when the Russian train (gauge 5 feet) entered European standard gauge (4 feet 8.5 inches). As Australians, we are all too familiar with, and embarrassed by, this type of problem (Qld 3 feet 6 inches, NSW 4 feet 8.5 inches, Vic 5 feet 3 inches). I was absolutely flabbergasted as the train entered a shed, was jacked-up and the bogies changed to the appropriate gauge! Our *In-Tourist* guide tried to stop me, but I was determined to photograph this engineering triumph – and I did. I just cannot understand why the Soviets were not proud of this and trumpeting it to the world!

We completed the world's longest train trip in the communist half of the still-divided Berlin. Our guide walked us through the Berlin Wall's Brandenburg Gate from communist East to the capitalist West Berlin. The overt display of capitalism on the western side of the border, and the raised platforms allowing people to gawk at the East Berliners were absolutely revolting. The Wall was to remain dividing Berlin for another ten or more years.

We rented a car and drove south to Bavaria visiting Ann-Marie and Konrad Bussler and my god-son Jan. They made us very comfortable, and we were able to enjoy some of the nearby towns. Passau, particularly, impressed us. We continued our road-trip giving particular attention to Switzerland rectifying the previous scant attention we had given it on our Grand Tour of Europe ten years earlier. We arrived in London on **27th August 1979,** the infamous date of the assassination of Lord Louis Mountbatten. We had been 'on-the-road' since 12th July some seven weeks in total and we needed to get to Canada quickly as the beginning of the academic year was looming.

Fortunately for us, Freddie Laker was pioneering low-cost airlines and Laker Airlines was proving popular. Laker had no on-line booking system, customers simply had to queue at a counter in Victoria Station. I queued for five hours to get the tickets for our family of four and saved about $5,000 on the regular price. Brits are good at queueing and so there was no tolerance of breaks from the queue. Pat arrived every few hours with food and coffee. I can't remember what I did about the toilet! We got the tickets and arrived in New York at 2:00 am after a trans-Atlantic crossing and picked up our hire car. Exhausted, I managed to drive through New York City on into upstate New York and eventually Ontario Canada where, several hours later, we all 'crashed' in the car. The kids were wonderful. So ended an eight-week saga replete with memories for a lifetime!

Travel Sickness

It may be a bit odd to write a short piece on sickness, but this is specifically about how things can go wrong when travelling and what was done to survive. **Odyssey Part III** illustrates how bad it can get and yet survive. **My *Annus Horribilis*** and **El Calafate** are two further 'survival challenges' recounted here providing survival advice.

In addition, this vignette links together snippets only briefly mentioned in other vignettes.

My *Annus Horribilis* 1981: My fortieth year!

In **Adventures and Re-Visits p 152-156,** I outlined a wonderful holiday in the **Greek Island Traditional Settlements** despite our travel agent's warnings. For us, it was a no-brainer. Of course, we went ahead with our plans starting with the trip to Greece.

It was time for the next part of the plan: **research trip to Moscow,** and finally back to Canada to finish my Master degree. In **Melded Family p 94** I described the scene: "in one of the saddest moments of my entire life, I stood on the roof of the Athens airport lighting match after match so Annie, Michael and their Mum might see me bidding them farewell as they returned to Canberra while I had to go on to Moscow and then Canada to complete my Master degree".

To get to Moscow from Athens I chose a train trip which I described in part in the vignette **Trans-Siberian Railway** p. 161.

"I chose to travel 'first-class' and found myself alone in the entire carriage. At each stop, poor peasants - some mothers with young babies - on noticing the obvious space, tried to board my carriage. It was sickening to watch guards, pushing them back using rifles as battering rams! Lenin, I'm sure, would turn in his grave".

The first few hours were very interesting up from Athens to Thessaloniki, touching on Macedonia and into Bulgaria. I had bought a ticket from Athens to Moscow so was a bit puzzled when the train came to a complete full stop in the capital of Bulgaria, Sofia. I was told to come back next day for the continuation train.

There was worse news. There did not appear to be any hotels. Using my feeble German, I discovered they do 'home stays' instead. Nursing a terrible migraine, I found my way to a home-stay offered by two maiden 'aunties'. They were nice to me recognizing that I was not well. Next morning after sleeping off the headache, they brought me breakfast in bed and I noticed the tea towel – Gold Coast Queensland! Might have been a present from an earlier intrepid Aussie traveller.

Next day, the train made it way up the west coast of the Black Sea around the area of Burgas and Varna – there is also an ancient Roman settlement in Nessebar in the region. All I could do was watch from the train window vowing to come back one day (and have not yet had the opportunity) as it continued on relentlessly into the Ukraine and on to Moscow.

Travel Sickness

Apart from the migraine, no real drama yet as I settled into a hotel familiar to me – the Hotel Metropole on Red Square in Moscow where I confirmed my research appointment for the morrow.

About five in the morning, I recognized some telltale pains knowing it could be the prelude to renal cholic. While I was dressing for my appointment, all doubt was dispelled as the so-called 'Prince of Pain' took hold. I knew I must get help quickly, but how? I decided to scream "Herz" on the bedside phone, and it seemed to work.

Not ten minutes later, an ambulance and para-meds arrived but my new problem was I didn't want to be treated for a heart attack. In German, I asked the para-meds to phone the hospital and ask for an English speaker to take the line. I explained that I had renal colic and that I needed morphine immediately. The para-meds readied a huge epidural needle filled with enough morphine to kill a horse (even a couple of horses). What alarmed me was their call: "genug?". My high-school German told me they were asking *me* to call the shots – when was enough!

Stretchered into the ambulance and off to the hospital, I was in for an education on the much-vaunted Soviet health system. A great boast was their 'Free Medicine' but, ah, 'You get's what you pay for!'. Obviously grossly underfunded, I observed a hospital out of a period-piece movie complete with ancient beds and vintage wheelchairs! Though adequate, the 'look' did not inspire confidence, but I drew the line when I saw the machine on which they wanted to X-ray me.

Travel Sickness

'Rontgen Ray' was imprinted on the machine. As a Physics graduate, I knew Wilhelm Rontgen was the inaugural winner of the Nobel Prize for Physics, in 1901! But this was 1981 and Western Medicine has learned to limit the X-ray dosage e.g. no longer using X-rays to get a good fit when buying shoes. I baulked. This was too much of a 'blast-from-the-past'. Next it will be Madame Curie.

I had had enough there were even bloodstains on the sheets. I escaped to a taxi and, in quick succession, reeled off the following: packed up at the hotel, phoned Dr Konrad Bussler in Germany, bought an Austrian Airlines ticket to Vienna and dashed by taxi to the airport hoping that the morphine was still working. My appointment was shot and I was going to escape.

The first four check points at the airport were OK and then came the dreaded "Nyet" at checkpoint five. The Austrian plane was almost at touching distance so somehow, I had to get through this. A notation in my passport from the Russian Embassy in Canberra had elicited salutes from border guards on entry to the Soviet Union two days earlier but would it work now? Maybe the hospital had dobbed me in for escaping? And junkies have been known to fake renal cholic to get morphine! Trying to look innocent, I waited and got a "Da"!

As the Austrian Airliner took off, the entire complement of passengers cheered, and I joined in lustily. (See a similar clip from the movie *"Argo"*).

Travel Sickness

It was Easter 1981 and Dr Konrad and Ann-Marie Bussler were at home avoiding the Easter traffic rush. They looked after me, cheered me up and got me on a plane from Munich to New York and Toronto.

Unfortunately, there was much more to come in my *Annus Horribilis* but there were some bright spots too. On the polar route after just crossing the Atlantic, the Captain asked us all to move to the right side of the plane for re-balancing while we looked out on the icy coastline of Greenland traversing it from north to south.

Dr Konrad had insisted that I seek medical treatment as soon as I got to Canada. I had a place in married-student accommodation, and I sought out the University Student Health Centre. I will never forget the Voiding Cystogram which I was subjected to which sent me into a shock reaction from iodine contrast dye – and the shock of waking up with about six doctors looking grave around my bed.

I was finishing off my Master of Management Science with vigour and enjoying student life too. (See: **Sailing the Great Lakes**).

Three quarters of the semester had flown by but, as part of my undertaking to Dr Konrad, I decided to have one of my moles checked by the University Health Centre. A day or two later, a single phone call reduced me to a dysfunctional wreck. It was the diagnosis "Malignant Melanoma", and the immediate summons to Toronto General Hospital for radical surgery. My problem was that an Australian doctor many years earlier had told me that, by the time this condition is diagnosed, it is invariably too late. It's a "bush-fire" he said.

My fellow students rallied around, driving me to the hospital, and arranging to sell my car for me. The Toronto General surgeon advised: "Get your affairs in order, you may have as little as six months but there is a specialist here that has some success in stimulating the immune system using a liquid medication that has to be stored refrigerated".

QANTAS was wonderful, bringing forward my booking home with a four-hour stop-over in Vancouver before the connection to the trans-Pacific flight. Again, my fellow students drove me to Toronto airport all organised within a week of the diagnosis. Flight attendants handled the refrigeration of the medication brought to me at intervals during the flight, as I was, by then, a semi-invalid.

Australian aborigines have a ceremony known as 'pointing the bone' By all accounts it is a very effective weapon; the one pointed at can even die! The 'bone' had been pointed at me and I was in a down-ward spiral.

Back in Australia, the University allowed unlimited sick leave as the months ticked by. At a time like this you find out who your real friends are. Only one fellow academic from the University visited me at home: Bob Mitchell, Head of School. Roger and Virginia Nairn visited and Roger's mother, a devout Catholic, initiated a novena.

My local doctor personally knew Australia's foremost expert on malignant melanoma in Sydney and arranged a consultation. Just over six months, with the clock still ticking, I had the consultation on 1st December, 1981 just shy of my 41st Birthday.

HISTOPATHOLOGY FORM

HOSPITAL NUMBER: B-4867-81
NAME: SCHMITT Peter   WARD: _____   DATE: 1.12.81
OCCUPATION: _____   AGE: 40   SEX: M   M.S.W. _____
REQUEST DR: _____   V.M.O. Dr. T. Davis

Lesion excised in May 1981 in Canada diagnosed as malignant melanoma

PUBLIC
INTERMEDIATE
PRIVATE

SPECIMEN: Review of slide of skin lesion reported by Dr. Wong, University of Waterloo Health Services, Waterloo. ONT. N213G1.

MACROSCOPIC EXAMINATION:

OPINION SKIN LESION (1535-81)   FILE IN CASE NOTES

One section only has been received. This shows scattered nevocytic cells and melanophages located in the upper reticular dermis. These cells are associated with a prominent lymphocytic infiltrate, and mild capillary proliferation. The nevocytic cells show a moderate degree of pleomorphism, but no mitotic figures are seen. The papillary dermis and epidermis show no significant abnormality. The lesion is well clear of the excision margins.

COMMENT

The histological features are those of a regressing nevocytic lesion. There is no definite evidence of malignant melanoma in this section, although it may not be representative of the lesion. All sections of the lesion should be examined in order to give an unequivocal report.

P. BULIPITT.
2.12.81

Dr Davis said he was sick of Canadians claiming high clear-up rates on malignant melanoma. He said:

"They have higher success rates because they 'over-diagnose'."

I said, "I should sue the Canadian doctors!"

He said, "No, just be thankful. Every single person in that waiting room would sacrifice a limb if it was necessary to get the news you got today!"

Travel Sickness

El Calafate, July 2011

In **Adventures and Places to Revisit** p. 145, I mentioned a broken wrist sustained earlier in El Calafate.

We had returned to South America specifically to visit Machu Picchu which had been isolated by a mudslide on our earlier visit. Our Australian travel agency, South American specialists, made special arrangements for us to make up for our earlier disappointment.

I had described our amazing experience of a day cruising around the Perito Moreno Glacier and, next morning, we had a mini-bus **waiting in front of our hotel** in El Calafate to take us on the next stage of the trip. I had a suitcase in my right hand and a back-pack on my back, just six steps down to the foyer and the waiting bus.

I stumbled a bit at the top of the stairs but failed to regain my balance which I later attributed to the shift in my centre of gravity caused by the backpack. I fell heavily left hand out to break the fall. The pain was excruciating.

Ann and the hotel staff brought ice for the bruising, but the pain was really bad. The mini-bus driver was standing by for us and I had to make a tough decision. I noticed that the only way to ameliorate the pain was to hold my left hand up vertically. I made the right decision: Cancel the bus, go to the hospital where just the look on the radiographer's face was enough – I didn't need to understand the Spanish. It was a bad break, and they would do a 'closed reduction' in the operating theatre after six hours. (I had eaten breakfast).

A cheery fellow wandered past my bed saying somewhat incoherently something like "Libs, libs?". Though initially totally flummoxed, I'm proud of the fact that I twigged what he meant in time to shout a good number to him as he was disappearing down the corridor. I had suddenly realised that we were in a part of the world where they are used to seeing Americans and Americans are still on the old weight measures of pounds (not kilos). And the key to the puzzle is that the abbreviation for pounds is 'lbs'. The cheery fellow, I twigged, was the anaesthetist. Body weight is the crucial determinant of the correct dosage, and I was nervous enough trusting a general anaesthetic in a regional South American Hospital.

I was also promptly visited by a representative of the travel insurance company who connected me to a helpful nurse in Sydney. I was impressed with the care they were showing by advising that I immediately terminate the trip and get on a plane back to Sydney. There was no way we were going to do that as this was our second attempt to get to Machu Picchu. [Subsequently, I was to discover the real motive for that insurance advice – their liability ceases immediately on return home as the travel would stop at that point].

We continued the trip, albeit in some pain. The further medical help I needed in Punta Arenas was first class – they were set up to service the expatriate workers on off shore oil rigs.

Still interested in the medical details: On return to Melbourne, I had an urgent open reduction complete with two titanium plates for life and three years of Complex Regional Pain Syndrome (CRPS).

The Trip that Didn't Happen

This was to be the trip of a lifetime– a voyage (*not* a cruise) – an adventure of 48 days duration with 45 ports of call: Embarkation in Singapore, passing through the Suez Canal, and ending up in London.

Our flight to Singapore was scheduled for Saturday morning 7th March 2020 embarking for a sail-away on Monday 9th March. In retrospect, we now can recall how crucial (and stressful) were those early days in March 2020. But first let me set the scene.

We had booked the trip, gradually paying for it over the previous eighteen months. I had carefully planned the shore-excursions that we would undertake in the 45 ports of call researching from a glossy book of hundreds of options recommended by the shipping company. For months, every Manly ferry trip to and from the office was a fun time researching options. The details of each one chosen were clipped and filed safely in a sleeve in a display folder.

Head Office wanted me down in Melbourne in the last week of February to brief 'stand-ins' who would cover my absence. My boss, who had a family wedding to attend in Asia on the same weekend 8-9th March, was confident that, despite some health concerns filtering through, "*Singapore Airlines* will sterilize their 'plane, and there will be nothing to worry about!"

As for any of our trips, we had also carefully stocked up on every conceivable medication that we might need over the extended period of the voyage. Given the news that had begun to trickle through about a 'flu-type virus emerging in China, we also bought some *Tamiflu* - the one and only virus medication - as it could be in high demand during a 'flu outbreak.

We did consult our doctor too. He advised: 'all clear' reassuring us that he was going ahead with his skiing holiday in Aspen also scheduled in early March.

'Be Prepared!', as the saying goes. We reassured our kids, though Annie and Samantha particularly had been strenuously advising against the trip throughout February. We had been told that the health scare would likely peter out at the latest by Easter. There was also the little matter of $25,000 at stake.

On Friday evening 6th March we had our bags packed sitting near the door ready for our *Uber* trip to the airport early on the morrow. We had one necessary last-minute trip to the chemist in Manly. Driving back, we needed to make the last of the goodbye phone calls to Annie as we had already farewelled all the other kids and grandkids. We were close to Annie's place, so we thought we would just drop by in person, but briefly, as we wanted to get a good sleep since we were already only hours from lift-off.

Amazingly, an hour later we had pulled the plug! Annie had taken us through a decision-making process where we, ourselves, made the decision to pull the plug. It wasn't easy, but it was a decision that we made ourselves. In the end you have to 'own' the decision else there is a strong tendency to resist a decision imposed.

Since I had already arranged time off work, we decided instead to embark on a road trip: South to friends in Canberra, Melbourne, and Tasmania; with a follow-up: North to family in Queensland.

All went well with the visits south until it came time to turn back for home. We only just made it out of Tasmania before they closed the border. By the time we got back to Manly, rumblings up north were enough to convince us to remain in self-isolation in Sydney.

And so began a long period of working from home (WFH). Granddaughter Anu and I are hard at it here!

My boss did go ahead with his trip to Singapore and onto a wedding in India. He just had enough time to get back to Melbourne, but his wife's slightly longer stay was protracted into months before she got out, under very difficult circumstances, via Dubai.

Our doctor went ahead with his trip to Aspen and got back from USA only after much trouble as COVID did *not* fade away as he had predicted it would. He had based his advice on experience with earlier epidemics that *had* faded away. The world was now in the grip of a pandemic for the first time in a hundred years.

We read the horror stories about how the States of Australia had closed their borders back then in the Spanish Flu pandemic. Stories of returned servicemen who had tried to cross the Victorian-NSW border by swimming across the Murray River after they had been de-mobbed and put ashore in a State other than their home State. **It couldn't happen again could it, or could it?**

The Aftermath

Our ship, the *Vasco de Gama,* did depart Singapore on schedule but accomplished just a single port of call- Penang. Being denied further ports, it headed to Freemantle and quarantine. Ah, was that always the cunning plan: keep reassuring passengers, but don't cancel the voyage thereby avoiding the liability they would incur. If passengers cancel, then be it on their own heads. We cancelled: so, it's our fault!

What about our $25,000?

Annie helped by immediately generating the appropriate paperwork to substantiate the claim that it would not have been safe for us oldies to have risked the trip. Instead of flying on that Saturday morning, Annie arranged a doctor's appointment and the appropriate letter.

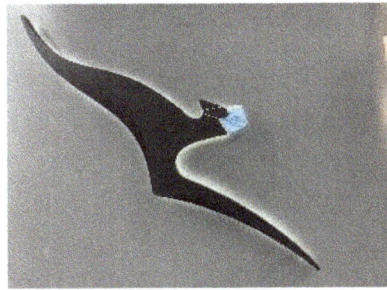

QANTAS immediately issued us travel credits.

Our travel insurance company came up with a meagre $5,000 only after an adverse publicity campaign developed by Gary. We also pursued the travel agency that had booked our voyage.

After some months the agency told us some news which looked bleak for our chances of recovering any more funds: Our ship, the *Vasco de Gama,* was operated by a UK-based shipping company which had gone bankrupt. However, the agency offered to make a claim for us on their own company insurance policy. They cautioned that the claim might take eighteen months to resolve, so we should not hold our breaths!

The Trip that Didn't Happen

In August 2021, I received a phone call from a nice young man who asked for our BSB and bank account number! I pointed out that I am not an idiot! He then began quoting a lot of details that only the travel agency could have known about us. I apologised and he said that he was conducting a round of such phone calls and that everyone had reacted to him in the same way as I had.

I gave him the details he wanted, and I waited 48 hours anxiously, and wow $19,500 dropped into our account – after a wait of about 18 months just like they said it might!

Expo67 Montreal

The 1967 International and Universal Exposition or **Expo67**, as it was commonly known, was a general exhibition, Category One Word Fair held in Montreal from April 27 to October 29, 1967.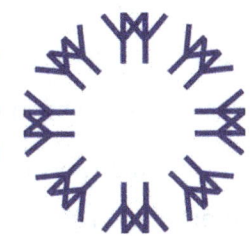

Expo67 was Canada's main celebration for its centennial year [Australia's centennial year was 2001].

It is considered to be the most successful World's Fair of the 20th century with the most attendees to that date - 62 nations participating. It also set the single-day attendance record for a world's fair, with 569,500 visitors on its third day. On the final day 221,554 visitors added to the more than 50 million (54,991,806) that attended Expo67 at a time when Canada's population was only 20 million, setting a per-capita record for World Exhibition attendance that still stands. Had it not been for me, Pat and her parents that tally would have been a meagre 54,991,802.

Our party of four visited Expo67 at the end of a two-week holiday which swung through the New England states, Boston and Salem Mass. (site of the witch trials) and Boothbay Harbour once the pre-eminent east-coast port over New Amsterdam (New York). I cringe now recollecting that I subjected the aged in-laws to the back seat of a Volkswagen for this trip! The swing through New England was focused on getting to Newport Road Island in time to witness first-hand the Australian Challenge for the America's Cup (12 Metre Yachts) by a boat named *Dame Pattie*. Lagging more than two minutes at the first windward mark Race-1, *Dame Pattie* was already dismissed as a serious challenger, ultimately losing the series 4-0.

I had always rated the Olympic Games at the biggest and best international gathering on the globe. The Sydney Olympics of 2000, for instance, rates as one of the best: the whole of Sydney was bathed in sheer rapture for two weeks. In Japan 2002, I was to discover the Football World Cup – an even grander international gathering over a whole month. Each of these events celebrate sporting prowess. So, for me, Expo67 represented a big discovery: a much larger, more profound international gathering showcasing the variety of human architectural and cultural achievements with a life of its own not for a few weeks, but for six months!

Examples of Architectural and Cultural Achievements Showcased
Pervasive throughout Expo67, was split-screen and multi-screen video technology. It was everywhere and, for me, this was the first time I had experienced it!

**Australia's Contribution:
The Grant Featherston 'Sound Chair'**
Pavilion designer Robin Boyd wanted to create 'the most luxurious and civilized salon' at the Expo. Grant and Mary Featherston were commissioned with the brief to design

an elegant wing-style chair that would be modern in appearance and able to accommodate an audio system to play programs about Australian life in both English and French. These would be narrated by well-known Australians.

Their design reflected the 'Spirit of Adventure' as well as the 'space age' aesthetic that underpinned the pavilion design. Australian-inspired colours were selected for the woollen upholstery: Eucalyptus (charcoal green) for the body; and colour-coded cushions of Eucalyptus and Desert (golden orange) to distinguish between chairs that offered the English from those that offered the French narration.

Boyd's idea was that 250 of these chairs would be informally arranged on luxurious, white woollen carpet to create a Salon-like atmosphere. Here foot-weary Expo visitors could rest, cocooned in individual sound shells, while listening to tape-recorded stories about the Australian way of life, arts/sciences and designed to place the human experience at the centre believing that the spatial and sculptural properties of a chair could create not only physical comfort but also psychological comfort. Featherston wanted the chair to belong to the occupant, not the building, that is, to look right in any position, and surround the listening sitter. Its shape should grow out of its function – be comfortable and produce a stereo sound perfectly. And, in keeping with the Pavilion's contemporary theme, the chairs should have an apparent casualness.

Credit must go to Robin Boyd deciding to feature these chairs as the centerpiece showcasing good design AND offering a soft-sell opportunity. Like me, anyone who spent days trudging from one pavilion to another, yearned for a turn in the sound chair to hear the Australian story in words and music.

When the Expo opened in April 1967 there were reports that vast numbers of people, up to 15,000 per day, were queuing to visit the Australian Pavilion to experience the 'soft spoken' chairs. In fact, over the course of Expo67, 20 million people visited the pavilion!

There are several stories about the after-life of the Expo Chairs. Some ended up being used in the Language Laboratories at Point Cook for the education of migrants and others went to the Parkes Observatory. McGill University also made innovative use of them.

At home, the Expo Chair won a Good Design Award and is featured at the Museum of Applied Arts & Sciences. It was developed as a commercial version released onto the market in October 1967. Named *Expo Mark II*, it was promoted as a personal stereo-sound chair that could be plugged into the radio, television, record player and tape recorder. Very Sixties!

In its most recent manifestation, it is fitted with SONOS sound; a selection of the Featherston collection is now available through *Gestalt* New York.

Footnote: Featherston came up with the idea to create a curve by joining two pieces of plywood together after playing with a folded tram ticket in 1950. He patented the technique. Fortunately, there were no iPhones or iPods then to distract him from essential contemplative time – the 'down time' that all creative people need. See *Vignette: On Boredom*

America's Contribution: Buckminster Fuller's Geodesic Dome
Buckminster Fuller, by his own appraisal, was a non- conforming misfit in the fraternity environment being expelled from Harvard twice: first for spending all his money partying, and then, after having been readmitted, for his "irresponsibility and lack of interest".

Expo67 *190*

Amongst his many awards, he was elected as an honorary member of Phi Beta Kappa on the 50th year reunion of his Harvard Class of 1917 from which he had been expelled in his first year.

The Dome spectacularly allowed enough room for the Expo monorail to take a circuit within and through the Dome itself.

The American pavilion stole the show exhibiting American cultural achievements. The dome was large enough to house within it several NASA space capsules that had returned to earth as well as satellites

Also showcased within the Dome were an exhibition of the development of the American automobile industry replete with many iconic vehicles and an exhibition of the motion picture industry featuring thousands of iconic photos and models.

Canada's Contribution: Architect Moshe Safdie's Habitat

HABITAT 67, or simply Habitat, is a model community and housing complex in Montreal, Quebec, Canada, designed by Israeli-Canadian architect Moshe Safdie. It was originally conceived as his master's thesis at the School of Architecture at McGill University and then built as a pavilion for Expo 67. Habitat 67 is widely considered an architectural landmark and one of the most recognizable buildings in both Montreal and Canada.

Habitat 67 comprises 354 identical, prefabricated concrete forms arranged in various combinations, reaching up to 12 stories in height. Together these units create 146 residences of varying sizes and configurations, each formed from one to eight linked concrete units. The complex originally contained 158 apartments, but several apartments have since been joined to create larger units, reducing the total number. Each unit is connected to at least one private terrace, which can range from approximately 20 to 90 square metres in size.

The development was designed to integrate the benefits of suburban homes—namely gardens, fresh air, privacy, and multi-levelled environments—with the economics and density of a modern urban apartment building. It was believed to illustrate the new lifestyle people would live in increasingly crowded cities around the world. Safdie's goal for the project to be affordable housing largely failed: demand for the building's units has made them more expensive than originally envisioned. In addition, the existing structure was originally meant to be only the first phase of a much larger complex, but the high per-unit cost prevented that possibility.

Sydney's Sirius Building

Designed in 1979, by Sydney architect Tao Gofers, Sirius echoed many of Safdie's Habitat design principles. It's Brutalist design integrates concrete block forms with habitable roof gardens. As

Habitat was, Sirius also was designed as affordable public housing fulfilling that function for 40 years.

Now, Sirius has been re-imagined. Working with and not against the building's Brutalist essence, award-winning Australian architectural firm BVN's transformative re-design work bestows Sirius with the prestige that its harbor-front address deserves. In addition to roof top gardens the penthouses have private pools with views to Sydney Opera House and Circular Quay.

The original 76 units have been retained, though some have been enlarged and a new amenities block incorporating pool, spa and gym has been designed. Sirius will become the second architectural icon here: the heart of the nation.

Expo67

Here, Ann is roaming The Rocks area of Sydney and this will be our new address.

Expo67 196

My Walk in the Woods

In the Bill Bryson classic **Walk in the Woods,** he documents a telling exchange he had with the inimitable Stephen Katz on finding him 24 hours after he had been lost while hiking the Appalachian Trail:

Looking at Katz's arm, a zig-zag of dried blood:

"Oh, that? It's nothing".

"What do you mean it's nothing? It looks like you've been doing surgery on yourself."

"I got kind of lost"

"Oh, Stephen, you didn't."

"I was thirsty, I plunged off into the woods. Not real smart, right?"

"No. You should never leave the trail, Stephen."

"Oh, now there's a timely piece of advice Bryson. Thank you so much. That's like telling somebody who's died in a crash: Drive safely now."

My Walk in the Woods at Cape Cod Massachusetts

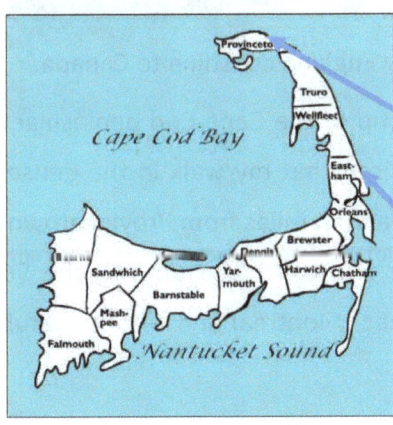

In the late afternoon, I stopped the car to hike across the mile or so to the shore of the Atlantic Ocean. The point where I alighted was actually here where the road was running east-west. I thought I was here where the road runs north-south. **I had left the trail!**

After a half hour trying in vain to reach the distant coastline, I turned back, sure that I knew where I was, and confident that the setting sun would guide me back to the road where I had parked the car.

After about an hour I was becoming distressed, and I sensed that something was wrong – maybe I was walking in circles. I was lucky to encounter a lone horse rider who 'saved' me pointing out the right direction that I should have been walking. My hour-long walk in the woods had been parallel to and set back just a couple of hundred yards from the very road that I was trying to find!

This is a beautiful part of USA, and I am sorry to say it took me 51 years to get back to this spot, aboard a *Windstar* expedition with Ann, Roger and Virginia starting in New York and up the New England coastline to Canada.

Provincetown, on the extreme tip of the Cape Cod peninsular, was one of the ports of call. I realised that my walk in the-dense woods could not have been more than ten miles from Provincetown (had I kept walking). The *Windstar* trip continued up into the St Lawrence Seaway through to Quebec, Montreal and the beautiful Thousand Islands region.

The Holy Grail of Yachting: America's Cup

The America's Cup began life in England as the Royal Yacht Squadron's £100 Cup, awarded to the winner of a race around the Isle of Wight. In August 1851 the race was won by the schooner *America* (after which the Cup was subsequently named) representing the youthful New York Yacht Club. The Commodore of the Royal Yacht Squadron, had invited the Americans to take part, and it would be the first foreign yacht to enter the race.

In a ploy repeated by the Australians in 1983 (see later), the Americans played up the radical new design of their yacht and hinted that they had a secret advantage below the waterline. Actually, it was the combination of a new hull design and less sail aloft that gave *America* the edge.

With this single victory, *America* transformed yachting into an international competition. The members of his ownership syndicate sold the winning schooner before returning home. They donated the trophy to the New York Yacht Club in 1857 under a Deed of Gift which stated that the trophy would be 'a perpetual challenge cup for friendly competition between nations'.

Australia's Sporting Prowess

Devoting the following 18 pages to a Yacht Race may appear somewhat of an overkill! In explanation, **the 1983 successful America's Cup Challenge represents a pinnacle in Australian sporting achievement**, one never likely to be bettered. Success in such a challenge had eluded all challengers for a period of 132 years stretching back in history to an era prior to the American Civil War!

Two other contenders for the crown of 'Pinnacle of Australian Sporting Achievement' would have to be:

Swimming Performance at the 1956 Melbourne Olympics

Finalists at the first Open Wimbledon Tennis 1968

Swimming at the Melbourne Olympics 1956

From just 13 swimming events in those days, Australia won eight. Next best was USA with two gold medals. In both the men's and the women's 100 metres freestyle, Australia scooped the medal pool winning Gold, Silver and Bronze. I well remember the hoist of *three* Australian flags at the medal ceremony.

My second cousin, David Theile won the Gold in the 100m backstroke joined on the podium by John Moncton winning Silver. Australia 1-2.

Wimbledon 1968

I attended these finals where Australia provided 7 of the 16 seeded players in the men's finals. Yes, really and Rod Laver (1) won the championship beating Tony Roche (15) – both Australians.

The New York Yacht Club's first defence of the America's Cup took place in 1870. Britain repeatedly challenged for the Cup, with one competitor, Sir Thomas Lipton, mounting five challenges 1899-1930. As the years passed, it was the prospect of breaking this more than a century-long winning streak that made the America's Cup so coveted. Britain and Canada were the only two nations to challenge for the Cup over all those years.

Australian involvement
Facing a 113-year winning streak, in 1962, an Australian syndicate headed by Sir Frank Packer and based at the Royal Sydney Yacht club challenged in *Gretel*. Although the Cup was successfully defended by the Americans, the competition was close, and *Gretel* was the first boat to win an America's Cup match race since 1930.

This taste of success, though limited to one race win in a best-of-seven series, spawned a run of Australian challenges. In summary: ***Dame Pattie*** 1967, ***Gretel II*** 1970, ***Southern Cross*** 1974, ***Australia*** 1977 and 1980, followed by ***Australia II*** in 1983.

1967: The *Dame Pattie* Challenge
Living in Canada from 1966 to 1968, I was determined not to miss the opportunity to witness in person Australia's second Challenge for the America's Cup. We drove down from Toronto to Newport Rhode Island in time to 'witness' the first race. I was to discover there was not much you could witness from any land vantage point in Newport

– you'd need to get on a boat to see anything! However, we imbibed the atmosphere of the yachting town of Newport for that first race.

It was not long before the news filtered back that *Intrepid* had beaten *Dame Pattie* (named after Prime Minister Bob Menzies' wife) to the first windward mark of the first race by several minutes. This effectively meant that it was *not* a viable challenge and so it proved to be the case. Disappointing, because Australia's first challenger *Gretel*, the 18th challenger in 1962, was acknowledged as the faster boat, though *Weatherly* defended the challenge 4-1 through superior crew work. There had been high hopes for the 20th Challenge, but *Dame Pattie* was not a good enough boat.

Observing first-hand the extreme wealth of Newport, I became convinced that it was pointless challenging for the America's Cup when the Americans here could clearly outspend any Aussies. I vehemently proffered that opinion whenever another challenge was being mooted (*Gretel II* 1970, *Southern Cross* 1974, *Australia* 1977 and 1980, even *Australia II* in 1983).

1970: Frank Packer Challenge with *Gretel II*

Australians returned in 1970 with *Gretel II* but again were unsuccessful. The *Gretel II* campaign was famously controversial, particularly when, having won a second race, they were stripped of their win by the NYYC. Future captain of *Australia II*, **John Bertrand**, competed in his first challenge on board *Gretel II*.

1974: *Southern Cross* and 1977 and 1980: *Australia Challenges*

Entrepreneur Alan Bond entered the Cup challenge process in 1974 with *Southern Cross*. Both *Southern Cross* and *Australia* failed in their three attempts, vindicating my opinion about pointless challenges. But they provided crucial training for the historic 1983 challenge.

Australia II

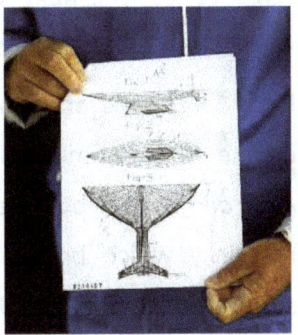

Alan Bond bankrolled the development of a new boat *Australia II* for a 1983 challenge. Ben Lexcen, who had also designed *Southern Cross* and co-designed *Australia*, designed the new yacht. Her outstanding characteristic was a completely new winged keel design. The NYYC embarked on a legal challenge to disqualify the Australian yacht. The boat was ruled a legal 12 Meter and allowed to challenge.

Back in 1851, it was the Americans who had played up the radical new design of their yacht and hinted that they had a secret advantage below the waterline and now it was the Aussies who would turn the tables. The 'under the waterline winged-keel' was kept hidden throughout until it was finally revealed to hysterical fans after *Australia II* had won the final race!

1983: Alan Bond's *Australia II* Challenge
Australia II, skippered by John Bertrand, lined up for the first race against the American defender, *Liberty*, skippered by Denis Conner, on 13 September 1983, but it was cancelled due to foul weather.

A successful start was made the following day, but *Australia II* was hampered by equipment failure. *Liberty* won by one minute and ten seconds. The next race was also marred by equipment failure, with Conner winning by one minute and 33 seconds. **[USA 2 – AUS 0]** Race three was abandoned as neither yacht could complete the course in the time limit, and was restarted the following day. *Australia II* won by three minutes and 14 seconds – a significant margin - which brought relief and jubilation to the Australians supporters. **[USA 2 – AUS 1]**

However, when *Liberty* won race four,**[USA 3 – AUS 1]** it seemed that it might be all over for the Australian campaign. *Australia II* would have to win every one of the next three races to take the Cup.

The fifth race started poorly, with the Australians giving the Americans a 37-second lead. However, the Americans lost this precious advantage due to equipment failure. *Australia II* won by one minute and 47 seconds. **[USA 3 – AUS 2]**

Race six took place on 22 September. Even if *Australia II* hadn't gone on to win the Cup, she still would have made history by winning this race. . **[USA 3 – AUS 3]**. It was the first time a defender had gone three-all, and it was the biggest winning margin recorded.

About 2000 boats turned out to watch the historic seventh race on 24 September, which disappointingly, had to be abandoned due to unstable weather conditions. Rescheduled for 26 September, the race started after only one postponement.

The Deciding Seventh Race

The Australians started well but lost their early lead. Things looked grim, with *Liberty* increasing its lead at every mark. Ben Lexcen couldn't bear to watch. He went below on the Bond's launch *Black Swan* alerted only by a change of demeanour of those above deck on the fifth, penultimate leg of the race.

The **Australia Museum opinion** about what happened:

'Two vital differences on this leg let *Australia II* regain the lead. Her spinnaker was set and held better than *Liberty*, and she was able to find a few extra lifts of wind that had eluded her rival.' (See also my opinion below).

Continuing….

'Once in the lead, *Australia II* was under ferocious attack from *Liberty* on the final leg. The American yacht tacked 45 times in attempting to regain the lead. **At 5.21pm *Australia II* crossed the finish line 41 seconds ahead of *Liberty*'.** [USA 3 – AUS 4]

For the first time in 132 years, on 26th September 1983 in the final race of the 25th Challenge, the America's Cup was wrested from American hands by Alan Bond/Ben Lexcen/John Bertrand's *Australia II*.

The Holy Grail of Yachting: The America's Cup

With the series locked at 3-3 going into the deciding seventh race, son Michael and I were glued to our TV set to watch the race at home in Aranda (Canberra),. We suffered as the defender *Liberty* led for most of the race. Hard to describe such depths of despair and disappointment after so much promise. Suffice it to say that some could no longer watch as *Liberty* closed in on victory.

It was at about 4am in Australia and glued to our TVs we saw Bertrand take *Australia II* wide to starboard on the penultimate downward leg of the race in an attempt to pick up a wind-shift. It worked! *Australia II* moved ahead of Liberty albeit out wider. Experienced match-racing yachties would say that Connor might have covered Bertrand's move but my guess is that he doubted the wisdom of going so wide as it would be difficult to cut back and round the final mark for the last leg of the race. Any time gained going wide would be lost in rounding the mark for the final leg. I will never

forget how Bertrand powered *Australia II* through the turn to that mark...that was the winged keel at work! I burst into tears.

My earlier, firmly-held opinion about the futility of challenging had just been comprehensively overturned.

As *Australia II* crossed the finish line, Michael Schmidt grabbed our Australian flag and ran into the front yard tying it to a tree. There has never, and there never will be, a greater sporting triumph in the history of a sporting-mad nation such as Australia.

Much of the nation had stayed up to watch the historic victory on television. (Those of us who had also borne the pain of the first four legs of the race were not impressed with those who had got up late just in time to see the final victory. We felt we had earned our ecstasy the hard way).

"The America's Cup, previously of interest only to the yachting fraternity, suddenly had a galvanising effect on the public mood. It was a never-to-be-repeated summer-long epic that wiped wars, politics, and economics from the pages of newspapers and brought the subject of boat racing into such unlikely places as the Oval Office of the White House", *(Lou d'Apulget)*

Dennis Conner successfully challenged the Australians in 1987 to regain the America's Cup.

Beyond Yachting: What can be Learned

The success has often been attributed to *Australia II's* winged keel and anyone who saw Bertrand drive *Australia II* round that final mark would have to agree. But there is a lot more to it than that. There are insights from this saga relevant way beyond winning yacht races!

Forget the pleasantries; We're here to win!

Bond, and many members of the crew, had been involved in the Newport-scene on three earlier unsuccessful challenges from which they had learned something. Typically, Newport identities host numerous social functions to fete the crew of the latest 'upstart' challenger. Bond saw that the whole point of these cocktail parties was to impress upon the challenger the futility of challenging such entrenched wealth and social status. The Newport hospitality offered to the honoured challengers was to out-psych them. On this his fourth challenge, Bond refused *all* such invitations announcing: "Sorry we are here to win the America's Cup!"

Public Relations Blitz and not so secret weapons

Bond's public relations team circulated stories of the secret weapon of the 'winged keel' which was kept covered by tarpaulins at all times guarded by maximum security night and day. It worked. There was an unsuccessful attempt by frogmen one night to breach security which simply added to the mystique and intrigue! The Americans became spooked by the winged-keel. So much so, that they tried (unsuccessfully) to have it ruled illegal.

The Holy Grail of Yachting: The America's Cup

Another successful psych-weapon against the defender and morale-booster for the challenger was a sound-boat equipped with massive 'ghetto-blasters'. It accompanied *Australia II* each time it was taken onto the course for training and races pumping out Men at Work's popular song: *I come from a Land Down Under*. Run through the lines in your mind – it would strike fear into anyone's heart: "You better run, you better take cover!"

Bertrand later described another psychological tactic. He trained his crew by accompanying their boat in training sessions with the sounds that a lead boat hears from a trailing boat. He said it was important for the crew to have ingrained into them that this is the sound that defines the status quo. The sound that a trailing boat hears from the lead boat is not the status quo and must create a tension until the status quo is restored.

He attributed his own capsize on the final leg of his gold medal Olympic race to the sound he heard as lead boat from trailing boats which felt not normal. He capsized finishing third as bronze medalist.

Apart from sporting prestige and national glory, there was a very serious money-making monopoly franchise at stake here in Newport Rhode Island - one that had brought in wealth for over a hundred years! Yes, there was a lot at stake. Bond too very much had 'skin in the game'. He was doing a lot of this on borrowed money!

Winged keel and a prayer: *The Australian* 26th Sept 2013

It was the race that woke the nation. And then gave it a day off work.

Thirty years ago today *Australia II,* backed by Alan Bond's millions - just short of $20m, to be more precise - and skippered by John Bertrand, sailed into sporting folklore off the waters of Newport, Rhode Island.

In the early hours of an Australian morning, Bertrand led his crew on the Ben Lexcen-designed yacht back from 3-1 down to break the longest winning streak in sporting history - one that dated back 132 years, to before the American Civil War.

Prime minister Bob Hawke then cover-drove sporting excellence magnificently over the top into sporting legend, clad in that iconic "Australia" jacket and almost too excited to sit in his chair at the Royal Perth Yacht Club. He framed the moment by declaring: "Any boss who sacks anyone for not turning up today is a bum."

Suddenly everybody liked sailing, and an Australia that had been down on its luck amid recession, droughts and bushfires finally had something to cheer about - so loud, in fact, its echoes refuse to fade.

> "I was in Ecuador with the government two weeks ago and as far as they go anyone who can organise a campaign and ultimately win the America's Cup - because they want things done in their country - they have a lot of regard for it," Bond tells The Australian. "So it still keeps you out there in front - it's the same with things I've been doing in Germany."

But it could have been so different. By Bond's own admission that final race in the best-of-seven series "was a win we shouldn't have had" - because despite the lessons learned from his previous campaigns there were still some enormous obstacles to success.

Ask Bond what his memories are of beating US skipper Dennis Conner and the Liberty crew of the New York Yacht Club and he'll tell you as much as the victory he remembers the technological challenges and the breakages his team had to overcome.

> "The effort we put into building two yachts, one conventional at that time for 1983, and one with the winged keel," he says. "We had to learn how to sail it and I think that was the most vivid memory: it just wasn't an ordinary yacht and it was very difficult to sail.
> "The crew got round it; they were a fantastic bunch of guys and we just got better and better as the series went."

But even with the commitment of his team, the Lexcen genius beneath the water and the cutting-edge sail technology above it, *Australia II* almost fell short. It had been engineered too light and after a gruelling elimination and final series was held together by little more than a winged keel and a prayer. It came down to the very last tack, says Bond.

> "There was a lot of wear and tear on the gear and we didn't have budgets like they have today, where they replace everything," he says. "I remember that gasping moment when it all came together; it was such a relief to win. Right up to those last tacks - those 42 tacks - we weren't sure what the girl had in her.

> "Which was proved the next day when we took it out for a photo shoot, and the first tack we did, we put the main up, the head of the main broke and down came the main, so we had one more tack left in it.
>
> "That's the sort of thing you vividly remember - if we'd put in one more tack we would have lost the race; he wasn't that far behind."

As it was, Bertrand and his crew sailed *Australia II* into our sporting hall of fame.

> "We only used to pay the crew - we didn't pay them at all, really - they just got a $12.50 pocket money; you wouldn't buy a beer for that, would you?" Bond says.
>
> "We did house them, clothe them and feed them but they went there because they were true sportsmen. They're terrific guys, you know you'd go to war with those guys. They're the blokes you want in the trench with you, they'll stand and fight and tough it out."

And as the party began on board *Australia II*, across the globe on what should have been dry land a recently elected prime minister found himself in the right place at the right time.

> "It was completely serendipitous; we'd arranged to have this cabinet meeting in Perth which was the next day," Hawke tells The Australian.

That night at the Royal Perth Yacht Club, Hawke remembers he was "nearly drowned in champagne". "I wasn't drinking when I was prime minister and I almost got full on the odour of the champagne," he says. "It was flying everywhere."

His next remark - like the win itself - is history; one of the greatest throwaway lines on political record.

> "It was completely unpremeditated and for all the brilliant things I've ever said since, none of them count - that's the one everyone remembers," Hawke says, laughing.

And for those wondering, despite only really answering to himself, Hawke did honour his own suggestion to Australia's bosses, and didn't get into too much trouble over it.

> "I was up all night watching the thing so, of course, they said there will be no cabinet meeting in the morning; we'll do that when we get back to Canberra."

Bond, now 75, maintains his love of sailing. Alongside the creation of Bond University - which marks its 25th anniversary in the coming year - he considers the 1983 campaign his greatest success.

But more than this there is a boyish enthusiasm for the sport - midway through an answer he stops to discuss the current ding-dong battle for the cup between Team New Zealand and Oracle Team USA, asking if I'd seen the latest race.

> "It's all over in 28 minutes or something; so much effort goes into it, I don't think you can put it in the arc of sailing," he says. "It's racing, yes, but not sailing."

Bond's love of the sport, his belief in Lexcen and crew drove him to four campaigns and ultimately to a glory he was very much part of.

> "Unlike what they're doing today, I was in the bilges of every decision that was made on that yacht, every sail decision, going right the way through," he says.

When talking to any of the crew of that 1983 campaign, references to what Bertrand describes as the boat's "Anzac spirit" are never far away. Their quest deliberately bore the trappings of a group of men going into battle.

> "We created the boxing kangaroo flag," Bertrand says. "Red gloves for aggression, the pumped-up chest for pride of a nation to take on the world. Whenever we won a race, we'd hoist our battle flag, and whenever we left dock at Newport, we bought the biggest loudspeakers we could purchase and would be pumping our battle hymn, Down Under."

The man whose genius outwitted the greatest technological minds of the US is not here to celebrate the anniversary. Lexcen died of a heart attack just five years after the win, aged 52. Lexcen is described by close friend Bertrand as a "truly wonderful man".

> "It was the fulfilment of his lifelong dream to design the winning America's Cup boat, there's no doubt about it," he says. "To me he was the Leonardo da Vinci of this country. Totally self-educated, he was at one with nature. He was in awe of what nature generates and its complexities; he was brilliant in so many ways."

And on the back of this brilliance, amid recession and natural disaster at home, a group of champions turned unlikely possibility into historical fact.

"It was a tough time, yeah," says Hawke. "But what they did was just so magnificent because for over 100 years every country in the world had been trying and nobody had been able to beat the Yanks and we did it ... it was fabulous."

Bond agrees his team, cut from regular green and gold cloth, showed a nation doing it tough that they could fight the good fight.

"There's absolutely no doubt it did," says Bond. "You see what this did, it showed people that anything was possible if you give them a reason to take on their own challenges in life.

> "The crew were very down-to-earth guys - Benny came up starting work in the railways - the public could relate to the people; they could relate to the effort.
>
> "It encouraged people outside the yachting fraternity; that's what really made it. The average guy, the average family, they were all supporting this yacht race when they didn't really know a lot about sailing.
>
> "So I think we captured that imagination, and that in turn spread through the economy," he says. "It was a real lift for people."

Where are they now?

John Bertrand (Skipper)- president of Swimming Australia, chairman Sport Australia Hall of Fame, chairman of the Alannah and Madeline Foundation and chairman of selectors for the Australian sailing team for the Rio Olympics.

The Holy Grail of Yachting: The America's Cup

Crew on *Australia II* after they won the 1983 America's Cup.

Syndicate chairman: Alan Bond - lives in London and Perth; business interests include diamond mines in Africa.

Syndicate executive director: Warren Jones - died 2002. Remembered through the Warren Jones International Youth Regatta and Warren Jones Awards recognising medical research excellence.

Designer: Ben Lexcen - died of heart attack in 1988.

Tactician: Hugh Treharne - operates a boat-servicing business in Sydney.

Navigator: Grant Simmer - general manager of Oracle Team USA in this year's America's Cup.

Mainsheet: Colin Beashel - competed in six Olympic Games and now runs Colin Beashel Marine in Pittwater, Sydney.

Trimmers:

Ken Judge - investment banker in Monaco, who has "never sailed since the last race of the America's Cup; been there, done that".

Skip Lissiman - executive officer of Swan River Sailing.

Rob Brown (reserve) - head of commercial operations, Royal Motor Yacht Club at Broken Bay, NSW.

Grinders:

Will Baillieu (injured, not on boat) - farmer in Redhill, outside Melbourne.

Brian Richardson - became head coach for Canadian, Australian and Korean rowing teams; now retired.

John Longley - former head of Fremantle Chamber of Commerce, now semi-retired.

Mast: Phil Smidmore - Etchell class boat-builder in Newport, Sydney.

Sewer: Peter Costello - director of Global Real Estate for Bain & Company, based in Boston; just retired.

Bow:

Damian Fewster - residential house builder in Perth.

Scott McAllister (injured) - runs shop in Fremantle.

The Holy Grail of Yachting: The America's Cup

Alternate helm: James Hardy - retired from the wine business and is "doing his thing, Gentleman Jim".

Coach: Mike Fletcher - former coach of Australian Olympic sailing team, who is now semi-retired.

Australia II: Sold by Bond to the Australian government; now at the Western Australian Maritime Museum, Fremantle.

Boxing kangaroo: Sold to the Australian Olympic Committee in the late 1980s; now appears wherever there's a sporting battle to be fought.

Sailing the Great Lakes

Phenomenal beer drinking capacity is expected of an Aussie abroad, particularly in a student bar - ask Bob Hawke. My fellow students and I meet in a particular bar every Thursday night come rain or come snow, and it is usually snow for this is Canada. Lubricated, we tell our stories.

The many Mexicans in our group generously proffer invitations to luxurious family haciendas back home. The Canadians all have grand entrepreneurial plans about which we enthuse whereas Australian counter-parts back home, in contrast, might target 'a good job' in a bank or the public service. When I have the floor, robust beer drinking and prowess in outdoor adventure is expected of me based on the hard won reputations of those who have gone before.

One Thursday night I oblige with stories of bare-boat chartering in Barrier Reef waters. I even flash a few choice photos of my own 20-foot keelboat under full sail. With the full spinnaker billowing out forward – fully forward so to speak – I exclaim "How sexy is that!" Many knowing smiles from the boys but the classmate alongside me, who has two full spinnakers of her own, looked puzzled – genuinely puzzled. Her remark floored me: "Do you mean the mast?" *Vive la différence!* Pub story-telling can get out of hand; it's not long before my class mates are busy organising a 50-foot bare-boat charter on the Great Lakes.

Sailing the Great Lakes

All eyes turn to me at the dock on Manitoulin Island^ϕ when the owner asks who will sign the charter documents and demands a one-hour proving test of seamanship. This is a huge step up from my 20-footer; the on-board electronics alone are a significant test for any grad student. We are a confident bunch, and we survive the test.

> ϕ Manitoulin Island is a Canadian island in Lake Huron. It is the largest freshwater lake island in the world

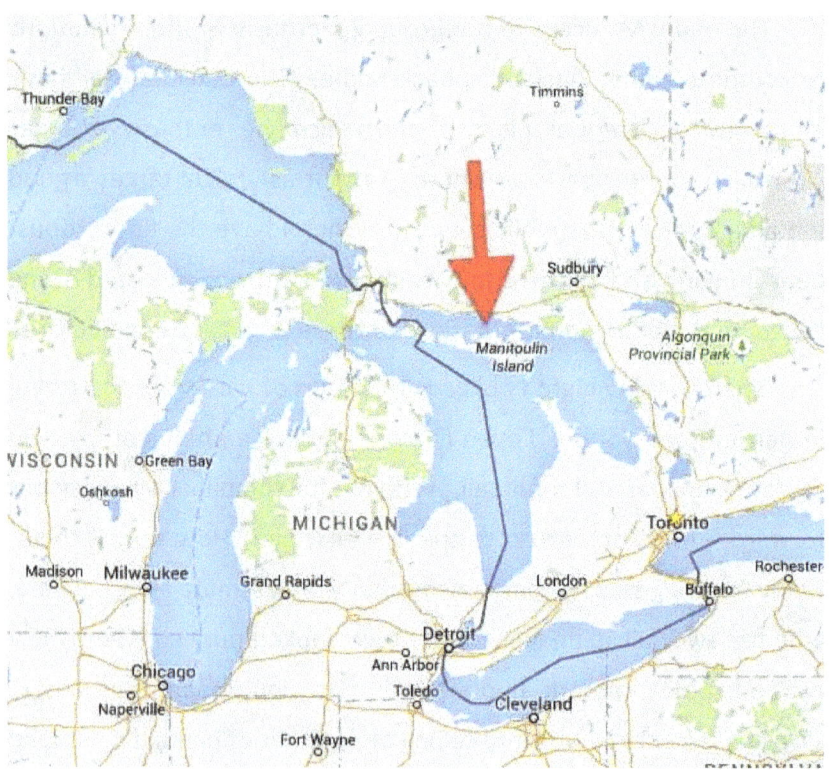

[The black line marks the Canada/USA border].

Sailing the Great Lakes

As my fellow students load slab after slab of beer, I realise that enforcing the 'drinking-starts-when-the-boat-ties-up-for-the-night' rule will be impossible!

Spirits are high as we set out but, not a half an hour out, we have a man overboard! Rafael's cap has blown overboard, and he leaps in after it. This is very cold Great Lakes water and sailboats don't have reverse gears. There are few more severe tests of seamanship than recovery of a man overboard within 15 minutes - the survival time at these temperatures - but somehow we achieve it.

I soon realise that I must detail three fellow students to watch over the electronics and relay depth-sounder information up to me on deck. The near disaster over the cap has a good influence and I am able to restrict frivolities until we tie up for a great all-night party.

Next morning, hung-over, we have the challenge of finding our way back to port in a pea-soup fog with almost zero visibility. I keep remembering that it is only I who has signed those charter documents! However, my student pals prove themselves on the electronics and we get back safely.

Later, on the bridge of the ferry taking us back to the mainland Tobermory where we had parked our cars, the captain continually sounds the fog-horn and tells me that there are still many yachts groping around out there in that fog. And thank goodness, none of my student pals seems to grasp that the outcome could have been oh so different.

Sailing the Great Lakes

Citycat and Kittycat

We round the bend in the Brisbane River and pull into the West End terminal and a uni student carefully loads his bike on board the Citycat for the crossing to the next stop - the UQ St Lucia terminal. This could have been me 55 years ago but the ferry we had in those days – somewhat like today's Kittycat – would not take my bike which was left where I would pick it up hours later after lectures. And that system worked a treat being the quickest way to get to uni from South Brisbane.

We didn't have helmets or combination bike-locks because I guess there was no compelling need to have them in those days. Sadly however, after two years, my system collapsed on the day when, on return to West End terminal after lectures, I found that my unsecured bike had been stolen!

Citycat is now into the waters between West End and UQ at St Lucia, and a name that had not crossed my brain for 50 years or more, screamed into my consciousness – Genevieve Spence. This stretch of the Brisbane River is personified by Genevieve in much the same way as a fatal accident site is personified, and often memorialised, by what had happened there. I am on deck astounded at my super quick recall of Genevieve's name, ah but the willowy Genevieve was a strong presence from my student days. Never achieving the fame of contemporaries such as David Malouf or

Quentin Strachan (Bryce), Genevieve was nevertheless the epitome of the new emerging independent educated woman of the 1960s and, being photogenic to boot, was a great favourite of UQ's publicity machine.

Genevieve's claim to fame was that she paddled a canoe across to lectures every day. I had noticed Genevieve on the water too and I asked her to the 'Commem Ball' at Cloudland.

We were in high spirits as I took her home to the West End after the ball. It was she who suggested we go out on this stretch of the river in her canoe despite our totally inappropriate dress and rather merry state of mind – ah, the confidence of youth!

She showed me her tricks for managing after-dark crossings following late lectures or parties. We twisted newspaper into torches which we progressively lit with my cigarette lighter.

Out on the water, an extraordinary thing happened – fish started jumping everywhere attracted by the light. Though our canoe was narrow of beam, about ten of the many jumping fish, each about 20cm long, ended up in the bottom of the canoe!

With her long ball gown and my dinner suit spattered with mud, we returned to shore and decided to divvy up the fish before going our separate ways. I was still living at home and it was, by now, very late, I decided the best place for the fish was in the kitchen sink as I collapsed into bed.

My Mum was used to my late nights and knew not to wake me, but I have chuckled many times since wondering whether she might have thought that those fish had come down the kitchen tap!

We ate the fish.

Fishy Stories (Part 2)

If you found the previous story a bit fishy, wait 'til you hear this one. Setting the scene: fast forward 15 years into the mid-1970s, and we are on the Crackenback River in the Snowy Mountains National Park and the main players are my best and longest-standing friend Roger Nairn and myself. If you are thinking about the movie *Jindabyne*, you are not that far off the mark. Thinking *Deliverance* is relevant too since Roger and I had set out with similar motives to those unfortunates. This is to be a back-to-nature, hunter-gatherer experience. Our surprise outcome, though was immeasurably better than theirs!

Personally, I'm not much of a fisherman due to the long boring waiting time involved but trout fishing was a different thing entirely. Trout fishing is all about stealth and quick action. The action takes place on the surface and is visible unlike other fishing where the action is hidden well below the surface. Another good friend Konrad Bussler, I imagine, would derive similar pleasure from his hunting expeditions.

The best chance of getting a trout is on the first cast into any section of the stream. Roger is a pretty competitive guy and I've been told that I am too so there is a race through the thick undergrowth on the river back to get that first cast into each new section of the stream.

We're exhausted from more than an hour of this when we round a bend in the stream and there before our eyes is a Mermaid! You might think we have been 'on' something illicit but no, so maybe we're hallucinating from exhaustion? We come closer and we notice this tall willowy apparition is practically nude! Have we died and gone to heaven?

No doubt observing our jaw-dropping astonishment, she speaks: "Would you like a fish?" We notice that she is actually wearing something but only waders which are the mark of the true trout fisherperson. She reaches down into her wet rubber waders to extract a trout which she offers to us!

Later, back at our ski-lodge, Roger is lucky to have me as an eye-witness to verify the story that he too verifies for me, ah, but our wives remain unconvinced.

Brisbane: 'River City'

Brisbane: "The River City"
[*cf* Sydney: "The Harbour City"]

What is the story here?

The story is the decision on the site of the new settlement in the Moreton Bay area. No doubt the impressive harbour site of Sydney would have been in mind when John Oxley's reconnoitring party came across the fresh-water sites of what is now Brisbane (on the Brisbane River) and Ipswich (on the Bremer). In fact, initially, they favoured the latter as the best site for a new settlement.

Perhaps Cairo (on the Nile) or the mouth of the Mekong and the seasonal inundations were not front of mind? But why ignore the evidence of left-over flood debris 100 ft above the current river level?

There is a big difference between siting on an ocean harbour and siting on a river mouth. Water levels in Sydney's harbour vary with the tides but within known bounds. However, in flood times, waters at a river's mouth may rise hundreds of feet above what is normal.

Brisbane is badly sited but, of course, it is too late to change all that now.

Brisbane: River City 228

Throughout the adventures detailed in *Odyssey I, II and III* earlier, I was kept grounded by a father-in-law who insisted that, in parallel with the fun and games of the European extravaganza, there would be a 'nod' to a responsible life sometime in the future. He insisted that this be in the form of a real estate purchase on instalments. He sourced a suitable purchase in the Brisbane suburb of Corinda arising from the re-zoning of the Presbyterian Montrose Home for housing blocks. (See later comment on the suitability of this sub-division!)

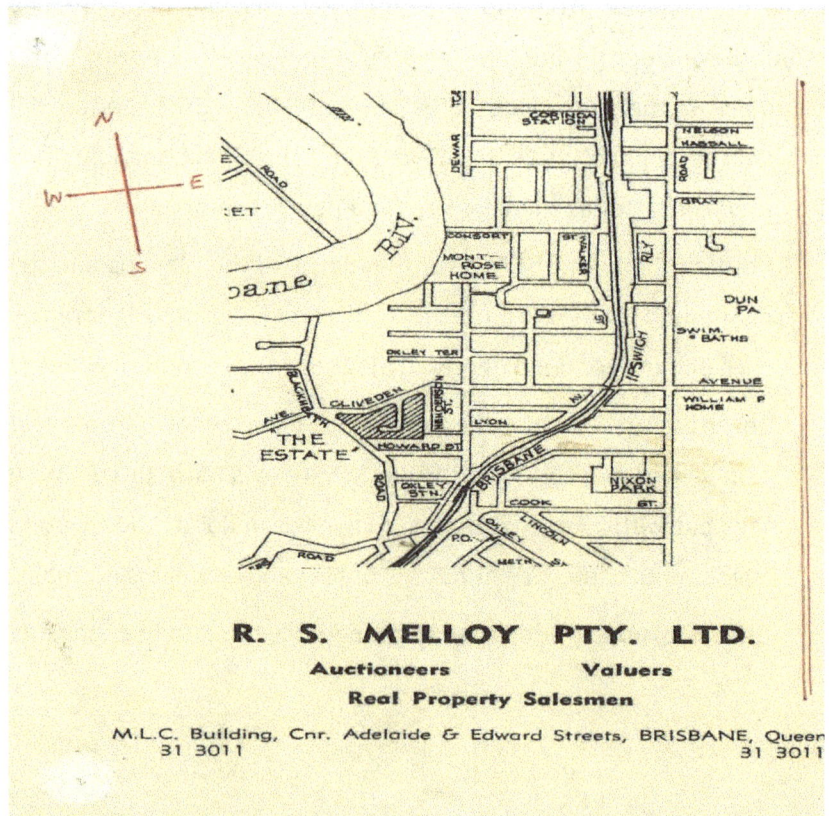

Father-in-law chose a 'dress circle' block overlooking the river. The block had a river frontage - highly prized in Brisbane! So much so that Brisbane even seems to have taken to calling itself 'The River City' in recent times. All I had to do was to put some money aside each month while 'splashing the cash' around Europe.

Note the standard of the Real Estate Brochures of the 1960s!

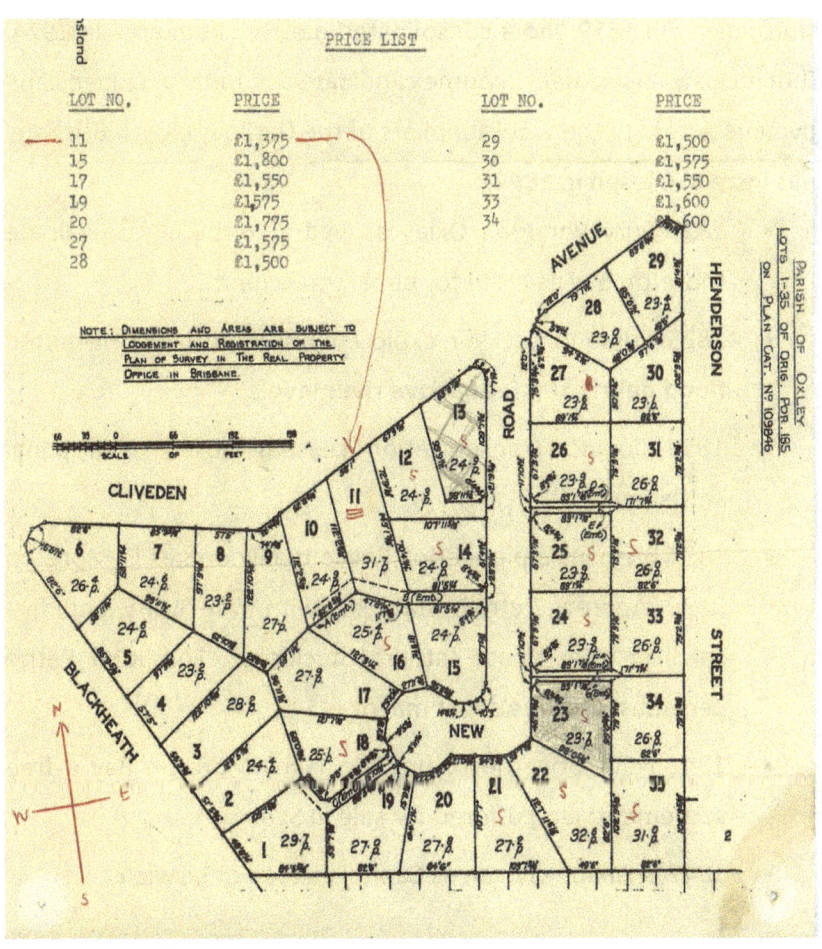

Brisbane: River City

Imagine the excitement, after almost three years on return to Australia, to finally visit the block noting its quality with considerable glee. So how did this, my first foray into the real estate market, turn out? Read on! But first I will start with a bit of history.

Brisbane History: In Summary

Brisbane's recorded history dates from 1838. The town became a municipality in 1859 and a consolidated metropolitan area in 1924. Though Ipswich had been a prime candidate as capital of Queensland given its access to the wool suppliers of the Darling Downs, Brisbane was instead chosen in 1847.

- 1823 Surveyor John Oxley arrived at Bribie Is to evaluate Moreton Bay as a site for penal settlement
- 1825 Edmund Lockyer explored Brisbane River. He noted **flood debris 100 feet above river levels**
- 1839 Convict transportation ceased; closed as a penal settlement
- 1837 Brisbane's pioneering Petrie family arrives in Moreton Bay. Andrew Petrie stays on with wife Mary and five children after penal settlement closes. Son John Petrie becomes Brisbane's first mayor
- 1842 NSW Governor Gipps proclaims Moreton Bay a free settlement: land offered for sale in Sydney
- 1847 Brisbane chosen as Capital instead of Ipswich

- 1855 Nearly 1000 German migrants arrive in Brisbane after political unrest and the introduction of compulsory military training; most settle in the Nundah area. Note: Lutheran stronghold even today
- **1893 Brisbane flood**
- **1974 Brisbane River flooding, the result of continual heavy rain from Cyclone Wanda, causes major damage across city**
- **1974 Corinda landslip**
- **2011 Brisbane River flooding**

Note the bold type above; Brisbane faced major flooding disasters in 1893, 1974 and 2011. The warning signs go back to 1825!

The Corinda landslip [from Wikipedia, the free Encyclopedia]
It was a substantial landslip event on a hill on the southern end of the Brisbane suburb of Corinda during the 1974 Brisbane flood.

The Corinda landslip struck **Cliveden Avenue** (Note: 11 Cliveden Av was our address), Oxley Terrace and Strathburn Street, located at the southern edge of the suburb of Corinda and extending into the neighbouring suburb of Oxley. The landslides in Corinda and surrounding suburbs involved "thousands of tonnes" of soil, with a section of Cliveden Avenue eventually being permanently closed to vehicular traffic. Geoscience Australia records that the landslip was over a distance of 1.6 kilometres (0.99 mi), with "ten houses evacuated, and 12 others threatened.

It was difficult to visualise any remedial measure that would provide a permanent, effective solution. At Cliveden Ave, there was movement of 30–100 mm per day on a slide 10 m deep". Land slid both onto Oxley Terrace and onto Cliveden Avenue. Several houses were demolished because "remedial measures were considered uneconomic".

Cold Comfort for the Distressed!
Alderman Gordon Thompson, a local Brisbane City Council politician, declared at the time that, within the landslip area, **"land that was being sold for home sites should never have gone on the market for that use".** The Presbyterian Church has carefully removed all references to the former location of the Montrose Home from the relevant web-site!

From the history lesson, it is abundantly clear that this, my first foray in the real-estate market, did not go all that well!

So, how *did* it all turn out in the end?
By early 1974, we had owned the 11 Cliveden Avenue for seven years gradually paying it off. Millennials will look at the price of £1,375 ($2,750) that we had paid in 1967 with envy. They'll say it's so hard for them now and we had it easy! Rubbish! That price was close to a full year's salary for a Queensland school teacher at the time.

Easy for us? No! Our target was to save, in just over two years, enough money to travel throughout Europe for nine months with no

Brisbane: River City

income in a brand new Volkswagen campervan (for which we would pay cash) **and also to put aside payments for that block of land.**

We saved like mad: no restaurants, no purchases, and trips limited to the Ontario/New York area. Each pay day for 2+ years, I subjected Pat to a savings conference plotting progress against our target with a red pin on a big board. She must have hated that!

"Europe on $10 a Day" was a popular guidebook at the time but we budgeted a savings plan recognising that we would generate a sustained spend of $20 a day because of European petrol prices!

And we did it! How? Two salaries; my salary from a good job with IBM which I then doubled when poached by Canada's largest stockbroker. [In retrospect, a bad career move, but a good cash flow move!] Also, it helped that North American salaries were high and the dollar was worth *four* Deutsch Marks at that time.

Meanwhile back in Cliveden Avenue

We discovered the joys of being absentee land holders of a vacant block, getting noxious weed notices from the Council every now and then! Not exactly what you'd want to hear about on a day on the Amalfi Coast! [Years later, in the Lofoten Islands of Norway, we got a SMS about a bathroom sink busted by a tenant. Or, the Coffs Harbour police calling me on the way to work in Melbourne about a different kind of bust - a hydroponic drug bust at our rental property with me the suspected Mr Big! See: *Vignette: On Remote Renting*].

By 1973, we had been back in Australia for a while and, with newborn son Michael, we were in the middle of an architectural build in Aranda at a total cost of $25,000. That was a lot of money in those days – about double the mean cost of a house in Canberra at the time. Again, millennials, it was a case of save, save and more save and also time to turn our Brisbane block of land into much needed cash. We sold it for $8,000 which was a top price as this was prime real-estate - a three-fold return on the $2,750 buy price.

Not long after Australia Day Weekend 1974
The whole of Australia had watched the horror of the massive Brisbane River flood over that weekend. About a week later, out of the blue, I got an unexpected phone call from a distressed young Brisbane man. Almost sobbing, he described what came to be known as 'The Corinda Landslip' (see above). And you guessed it: he was the recent buyer of our 11 Cliveden Avenue land and, as he put it, the block had been reduced to air-space.

My helpful(?) advice was: "You'll need to claim on insurance".

"You can't insure a block of land!" he sobbed.

However, sympathetic I might be, I must confess that rattling through my brain was the phrase: "Better you than I, Gunga Din!" But of course you'd never blurt that out! "You need to contact the Queensland Government for flood relief funds", was the best I could come up with.

So, by the narrowest of margins, we had dodged a bullet – perhaps making up for the hits we had had a few years earlier in Afghanistan.

It was all so predictable: Recall 1825, 1893, and then 1974. That's a 1974 aerial photo of the Corinda stretch of the River!

It couldn't happen again, could it? The vocal warmist Tim Flannery, in the later stages of the big millennium drought, predicted: "It will never rain like we have been used to. The dams will never fill again". **And then came the next big Brisbane River flood of 2011** washing away his prediction. [Another of his predictions about melting ice raising sea water levels, was enough to panic two Hawkesbury waterfront owners into selling, no doubt at the right price, to, you guessed it, Mr Flannery!]

The whole of Australia is excited about the successful Brisbane bid for the 2032 Olympic Games. So, we have about ten years to build another dam, Queenslanders!

It couldn't happen again, could it? Or could it!

Brisbane: River City

On Remote Renting

Any phone call from the police is extremely unsettling particularly when they insist on withholding details. It was mid-2006, we had been back in Australia nearly three years and I was walking up from home in William St, Melbourne to catch a Collins St tram to work.

"Are you the owner of a property, 7 Sapphire Place, Sapphire?"

"Yes *(quizzically)*"

"You should know there has been a police matter at the property, Do you know anything about that?"

"No, what's the problem?"

"I cannot reveal that Sir, it is an on-going investigation."

"Looks like I need to fly up to Coffs Harbour?"

"Yes, Sir"

About six hours later, I arrived at the Coffs Harbour Police Station, introduced myself and asked:

"Now, what's this all about?"

"We can't tell you Sir; it is an on-going investigation."

"Hey, I have flown all the way from Melbourne, now what's this all about?"

"It's a drug related matter, and it is an on-going investigation."

"*(increasingly agitated, expletives deleted)* What's going on?"

"Can't tell you anything; You could be Mr Big!
Why don't you go to the property and see for yourself, Sir."

On Remote Renting

On arrival at the property, I learned that our tenant had vamoosed! An electric pump for pumping rainwater into the garden was gone. Inside there were many unrepaired items like broken toilet seats, window catches and worn-out tap washers. There was evidence of a quick exit such as coins strewn in the garden.

The mystery was finally cleared up when the police visited and showed us how the electricity metre had been bypassed. We were able to piece together the plot. The double lock-up garage had, underneath the concrete slab, a large concrete water tank that collected rainwater from the roof and a pump to distribute it. The former owners had been keen gardeners and were the kind of people who would display a *'ONLY RAINWATER IN USE'* sign in the garden. Our site was ideal for hydroponic marijuana: a double lock-up garage; an independent water supply which hid abnormal usage of water; a bypassed electricity metre which hid abnormal usage of electricity; a remote landlord and an ineffective local Property Manager who did little other than collect the rent!

Clearly, the production side was impeccably nailed down but there's more. The tenant had the retail side sewn up too. I had met him on home-leave trips, and he presented well as the Manager of the Coffs Harbour *Hog's Breath* fast-food franchise. I imagine he sold to trusted customers there. So good was the system he had in place that it worked a treat for more than five years. So, what went wrong? Just one mistake selling to an under-cover cop, perhaps!

On Remote Renting

We had been renting to him and his partner for years dating from our last few years in Malaysia. The Property Managers had always reported favourably. On home leave trips, I made a point of visiting the property. More than once on these occasions he told me he would like to buy the property. I guess it was ideal for his purposes, but we were planning a development there so it was not for sale.

I am embarrassed now realising that on every one of these occasions I would have walked right past the locked-up garage and never sensed anything. But the biggest hint of all was his model tenancy – unlike most tenants pestering the managing agent and owner for maintenance items and 'improvements', he never uttered a peep of complaint. I know now that is a red flag indicating that something may not be quite right just as a manager should be suspicious of employees who never want to take holidays.

Such are the trials and tribulations of the remote absentee landlord!

On Remote Renting 240

On Boredom

From Rick Steves Travel Book: **"The Church in the Rock"**, [Our visit: Helsinki Finland 3rd April 2014]

> **"Grab a pew...Gawk upward .....and ponder God. *Forget your camera*. Just sit in the middle, ignore the crowds, and be thankful for peace...[there is an air-raid shelter under your feet that can accommodate 6,000 people]."**

Steves is right, everyone who's ever been there "felt something".

At the Church in the Rock, we thought of each and every one of you - our family - enough to select an *aide memoire* for each of you.

Though Rick Steves probably didn't realise it, he was inadvertently channelling the German Philosopher Marin Heidegger's treatise on boredom:

> "Profound boredom, drifting here and there in the abysses of our existence like a muffling fog, removes all things and men and oneself along with it into a remarkable indifference. This boredom reveals being as a whole."

> "Common passive ways to escape boredom are to sleep or to think creative thoughts (daydream)."

> "Boredom also plays a role in existentialist thought. In contexts where one is confined, spatially or otherwise, boredom may be met with various religious activities partly because boredom may be taken as the essential human condition to which God, wisdom, or morality are the ultimate answers."

Heidegger, in 100 pages on boredom, defined the most extensive philosophical treatment ever of the subject. In particular, he focused on waiting at railway stations as a major context for studying boredom.

Though I am no Heidegger, I am a regular observer of the human condition though my focus has not been on railway stations but on tram trips during the twenty minutes every morning and evening to and from my work in Melbourne.

I have made a few observations during these tram trips:

> Almost all tram travellers in the period 2004-09 were plugged in like zombies to their *iPods*
>
> Then it all changed. Out came the *iPhones*: Hunt and Peck..click, click, click. As Simon Baker says, (in an old ANZ Bank ad), to his fellow air-traveller chained to his lap-top computer: "Every minute counts, huh!"
>
> And, I have been known to say: "Don't you get enough of that at the office?"

I fear for the productivity of the nation, when a generation fills its time with drugs such as ice and *Facebook* (though not a drug, just as addictive). Both are productivity killers. There are other Planet Earth dwellers who are more determined, more focused who are not wasting their lives on *Facebook* and ice. I fear we will be no match in competition with them.

I fear that there is no time left for the brain to **process**. There are lots of **inputs** coming in continuously and then the **outputs**, but no processing time – no existentialist time – no time for creative daydreaming – no time for new ideas.

While in Helsinki, we experienced another profound existentialist experience aided by the Sibelius monument.

For my father, visiting Helsinki fifty years earlier, the Lutheran Cathedral would, no doubt, have served that purpose for him.

On Books

Not often would a single line from a drama presented on TV remain firmly in one's mind forever. **'We read to know we are not alone'** is the line that playwright Nicholson attributed to C.S. Lewis in *Shadowlands*. It resonates and will stay with me forever.

The context is the period of Lewis's role as Philosophy Tutor and Fellow at Magdalen College Oxford. In *Shadowlands* we see him hurrying, late we presume (and under-prepared), to his office to keep some appointment which he seems not to recall exactly. A postgraduate student, spotting him rushes to confront him in his office about the tutorial which Lewis had missed.

Gathering his thoughts, Lewis vocalises this single line exhorting the student to ponder and write an essay around it. It is a profound thought of great man of English literature found worthy of a place in Poets Corner in Westminster Abbey.

Why this scene and that line so resonates is perhaps because of my personal experience of university life which was a bit like that – not Oxford - but replete with real talent in the days when only 1 in 40 high school achievers enjoyed the privilege. And, as an 'old-school' academic myself for years and years, I had my fair share of students scurrying after me about things I had forgotten. Again, it wasn't Oxford, but it was a copy of that university-model.

Nowadays, things are perforce different and for good reason in the age of mass tertiary education.

Less profound was an experience I had in the 'waiting room' just before a recent ZOOM conference call. I was asked how things had been going for me over the weekend in Sydney and I proudly mentioned I had just finished the Bill Bryson's hilarious book *A Walk in the Woods.* "Have you read any of his books", I asked.

I was gob-smacked at his answer: "Peter, you could count the books I have ever read on the fingers of one hand. I am far, far too busy keeping up on the technical literature". He is in the professorial ranks with speciality in IT. And he is obviously very **focused** – a topic I pick up again in the *Vignette On Music* following.

Then there is the issue of **just what is it that we read**. In March 2021, demographer Bernard Salt, in his weekly article in *The Australian*, made some observations about reading habits. Though I know several of these will annoy some people, particularly the ladies, I must say they resonate enough with me to reproduce them here. As the saying goes these days: "Whatever, Just sayin'….."

> **Fact Aficionado Society: I don't read fiction and I'm not alone**
> Bernard Salt, March 19, 2021
> Young woman in a restaurant reading a book.
>
>
>
> Let me tell you about a secret society that shall remain secret not a moment longer. I am talking about those of us – including me – who prefer fact over fantasy, non-fiction over fiction.

On Books

It is true that some who claim membership of the Fact Aficionado Society like to make comments such as: "We are guided by the science." But this is base-level stuff because full-on aficionados take their fact-fancying a whole lot further. Members of the group share a common trait: they don't read fiction. A work of fiction may well be finely crafted, but it's the creation of an author's mind.

Now I know what you're thinking. Some works of fiction are so powerful, so exquisite, that they deserve to be read in full. I have yet to come across any such work. I try. I start reading the first page but by the top of the second page my fact-demons start whispering in my ear: This is all made up. It didn't happen."

I could never join a book club – where, I gather, the idea is to read a novel and then discuss as a group what these made-up characters may have thought about a particular made-up dilemma. No thank you.

The usual criticism is that those who do not – or cannot – read fiction lack creativity. I don't accept that at all. I read newspapers voraciously (mostly online these days), which exposes me to views that are vastly different to mine. I am interested in how people think; I think through counter-arguments. I read non-fiction books, most recently Origins: How the Earth Shaped Human History by Lewis Dartnell, which shows how geology influenced human settlement. I loved the evidence-based storytelling of Sapiens: a Brief History of Humankind by Yuval Noah Harari. I listen to podcasts such as the BBC's In Our Time with Melvyn Bragg, each episode a deep-dive with genuine experts into a different subject. I like facts, ideas and opinion that leave me enriched for the time I've invested.

I like the data reports of the Australian Bureau of Statistics. These are anything but dry and lifeless. Especially those that reach back over time. This is why the census is so important; it's like a dipstick that takes a reading of the Australian people at five-yearly intervals. We can see where we've been, where we are; perhaps where we're headed. Did you know, for example, that in 1971 the average age at first marriage for an Australian woman was 21 and for men 23, whereas today the equivalent years are 29 and 31? Back then a young woman was likely to announce her engagement on her 21st birthday. My, how we've changed.

But the secret society of fact aficionados doesn't restrict itself to data, it extends to maps. I will happily read a street directory of any city, and recently discovered online the maps of Charles Booth, a social researcher who mapped London poverty in the late 19th century. The insight isn't so much in seeing in exquisite detail the cadastral morphology of the world's greatest city at the time, or Booth's social stratification (from the criminal and vicious to the wealthy and upper class) but rather his breakdown of London into parishes of the Anglican Church. A century later, we break down the city into postcodes for delivered mail. How will cities be structured in another century, when both religion and delivered mail might have receded further?

All this creative interpretation stems not from novels and plays but from data, from facts. In some ways I think creative thinking is part of the human condition. It just surfaces differently in every one of us — including those slightly odd, fully fledged members of the Fact Aficionado Society.

On Books

My Reading Habits

As a typical academic, I have a vast personal library split between our home and our beach house. I have a particular interest in maritime history e.g. the Batavia 'mutiny' off the coast of Western Australia and, of course, the Mutiny on the Bounty. I have a copy of practically every book published on these mutinies where the latter is but a 'Sunday School Picnic' in comparison with the former. In fact, the former is so bad, that it shakes faith in humankind and astounds in the extent of the barbarism of which humans are capable.

I have noticed that the Batavia story is generally well known to Western Australians but not so well known to us Easterners. That may have something to do with the versions of history taught in the schools.

My interest in the Batavia story will take me on a trip to what is now an archaeological site where I am told I will still be able to see the impression that the ship's bow made in the coral reef on impact.

As for the Bounty story, the really compelling part of it is the story that unfolded on Pitcairn Island after the mutiny. How do you establish some form of law and order amongst a group of mutineers all of whom have already committed a capital crime? The answer to that question is that you can't! All but one of those mutineers died at the hands of the others in a series of murders. And what triggered the murders?

In a word: Women. It was the untimely natural death of one them that led to an imbalance in the numbers of males and females which then triggered a series of murders. This fascinating part of the *Bounty* story came to my attention reading R.B. Nicholson's The Pitcairners more than 40 years ago.

The major part of the Bounty story is the survival of Bligh and his men sailing an open boat from Tahiti in the Pacific to Indonesia. This is the supreme maritime achievement story of all time: A 47-day journey of over 3,600 nautical miles through stormy seas in an open boat with freeboard of less than 10 cms. Apart from the maritime achievement, it is a story of Bligh's leadership. Published in 1928, *Bligh of the Bounty* reproduces large sections of Bligh's journal of the odyssey. That the journal survived is itself a miracle wrought by Bligh himself holding it close to his chest throughout the entire ordeal.

Rob Mundle's 2010 publication *BLIGH Master Mariner* also reproduces much of Bligh's journal, and he dedicates his book:

> *To those individuals who, like Bligh,*
> *have stood proud through adversity,*
> *slander and ridicule and gone on to*
> *achieve great things*

Aldous Huxley's *Brave New World* is another special favourite. Huxley expertly foresaw and chronicled the world to come! Edward Woodward did an audible book version - scary stuff!

The Music

Benjamin Britten's Hymn to St Cecilia

Henryk Gorecki's Symphony of Sorrowful Songs

Verdi's Requiem

Vaughan Williams' Dona Nobis Pacem

Brahms' Ein Deutsches Requiem

And throughout all Eternity
I forgive you, you forgive me.
As our dear Redeemer said:
"This the wine, and this the Bread."

William Blake

and The Poetry

W H Auden

Walt Whitman

John Bright in a speech in the House of Commons

The Latin Mass

Summing it all up: Time to think

Sheila Handcock on John Thaw

Mikhail Gorbachev on his beloved wife Raisa

The Music

Benjamin Britten's Hymn to St Cecilia:

The scene is set in **May 1962**, the inter-Varsity Choral Festival and Sydney University Musical Society has the stage at the **Great Hall of Sydney University** and a soprano is leading the refrain:

> Blessed Cecilia, appear in visions
> To all musicians, appear and inspire:
> Translated Daughter, come down and startle
> Composing mortals with immortal fire.

She is singing like an angel, despite, sadly, gossip to the contrary. But it really does not get any better than this. Despite my tender years, I have a profound sense that this is so, that this is a moment to stop the clock.

It's W H Auden's poem that forms the libretto and Britten has 'raised' the key of the music at the word 'translated'. 'Immortal fire' is one of those onomatopoeic phrases like 'eternal light' (see below) and Britten gives the words to the bass baritone to provide the emphasis.

Auden's poem continues in a verse that had special meaning in regard to his relationship with Benjamin Britten but it resonated with me too. It seemed to mark the inevitable 'loss of innocence' and with it the demands of responsible adult life which graduation would, all too soon, mean for me. That's why I wanted to stop the clock.

The theme of loss of innocence is the subject of the whole of the first chapter of these memoirs. (See **Odyssey Part III**)

O dear white children casual as birds,
Playing among the ruined languages,
So small beside their large confusing words,
So gay against the greater silences
Lost innocence......

The Symphony of Sorrowful Songs: Henryk Gorecki (1933 -)

While St Cecelia was the muse for Britten and many other composers, the Polish composer Gorecki was driven by an inspiration that is so strong and so elemental that it speaks to the very essence of what it means to be a human being. This work of art goes way beyond another horrible war story addressing a universal story - the agony of the mother of a child taken.

The first and the third movements are written from the perspective of a parent who has lost a child while the second movement from that of a child separated from a parent. The theme is of motherhood and separation through war.

Gorecki learned of an inscription scrawled on the walls of a Gestapo prison in southern Poland and it was this inscription, framed in the second movement, which inspired the entire work. The words were those of an 18-year-old girl incarcerated in September 1944. It read **"O Mama, do not cry"**.

The composer said he was irritated by masses of inscriptions such as "Murderers", "Executioners", "You have to save me". Adults had obviously written these words but amongst it all was an eighteen-year-old girl, almost a child, writing her words. She does not despair, does not cry, does not scream for revenge. She does not think about herself, she thinks only about her mother, because it is her mother who will experience true despair.

Queensland University Choral Society (QUMS)

There were many times in those QUMS days that I would have stopped the clock. The yearly inter-Varsity Festival, brought together 300+ young, committed, eager voices. I always joked that there were a lot more sopranos and altos than there were baritones and tenors, so the choir did have other compensations. I met Pat in the choir.

Some of the highlights were: being chosen to stand alongside a great chorister who was to become a lead baritone with Opera Australia – John Pringle; singing in a 300-strong choir accompanied by Melbourne Symphony Orchestra performing Verdi's Requiem; having Colin Brumby (noted composer) as our full-time conductor.

Verdi's Requiem

How we hated this 'Italian' music in the early rehearsals, but as we got into it, we realized we were privileged to have this opportunity. Now, with an understanding of the music and the libretto which can only be grasped through performing it, I would travel 1000 km just to hear a live performance!

Obviously, we became very familiar with the biblical texts and one of our favourite party tricks was to quote long sections of the Latin mass, to the amazement of our non-choral friends. Our generation had studied Latin at school, and we had a love of it particularly of phrases such as *'lux perpetua'* (see below). In addition, we stumbled into some wonderful poetry though the librettos.

Vaughan Williams: Dona Nobis Pacem

Again, we hated this 'modern' English music in the early rehearsals, but as we got into it, we realized we were privileged to have this opportunity, again in the Great Hall of Sydney University, as part of a 300-strong choir. The libretto was my introduction to the poetry of Walt Whitman in the fourth movement: **Dirge for Two Veterans.**

> Lo, the moon ascending,
> Up from the east the silvery round moon,
> Beautiful over the house tops, ghastly, phantom moon,
> Immense and silent moon.
>
> O strong dead-march you please me!
> O moon immense with your silvery face you soothe me!
> O my soldiers twain! O my veterans passing to burial!
>
> What I have I also give you.
> The moon gives you light,
> And the bugles and the drums give you music,
> And my heart, O my soldiers, my veterans,
> **My heart gives you love.**

Vaughan Williams also incorporated parts of the famous speech delivered by John Bright in the British House of Commons after the War:

> *The Angel of Death has been abroad throughout the land; you may almost hear the beating of his wings. There is no one as of old . . . . . to sprinkle with blood the lintel and the two side-posts of our door, that he may spare and pass on.*

Few politicians have expressed the profound, the unspeakable, as well as John Bright has done.

Brahms Requiem:

Herr, lehre doch mich dass ein Ende mit mir haben muss

I like the literal transliteration:
> Lord, teach me that (you), an end with me, must have!

The correct translation is:
> Lord, make me to know mine end, and the measure of my days.

Denn alles Fleisch es ist wie Gras und alle Herrlichkeit des Menschen wie des Grases Blumen. Das Gras is verdorret und die Blume abgefallen.

The correct translation is:
> For all flesh is as grass, and all the glory of man as the flower of grass. The grass withereth and the flower thereof falleth away.

Requiem aeternam dona eis, Domine et lux perpetua luceat eis.

> Eternal rest grant them, O Lord,
> and let perpetual light shine upon them

The Music

Those beautiful Latin words: Et lux perpetua luceat eis

How many times have I been privileged to sing **those beautiful words** from the Catholic Requiem Mass! It **is** all about the light, isn't it? I spoke about it at Samantha's wedding: It's about the light! Even as we struggle to cope with the darkness in our lives. This simple nursery song nailed it!

May the Light that Shines on me,

Shine on the Ones I Love

Summing it all up: What does it all mean?

It is probably appropriate that, in this last chapter, to reflect on some of the many quotes in this chapter from a variety of sources, biblical and poetical. Perhaps these words may strike a chord with the reader? However, they are not my words. These are words that I have been privileged to discover through a trait not much valued these days – **a lack of focus**, but more on that later!

First, a word about some of the quotations I've selected for this chapter. The quotes in German from Brahms "Ein Deutsches Requiem" have biblical origins but they have really spoken to me for at least the last 55 years. And those beautiful words *"Et lux perpetua luceat eis"* are hard to sing without breaking into tears. Whether incorporated into Mozart's, Faure's or Verdi's Requiem, the composers invariably set these special words to best music.

Particularly in management circles, we hear a lot about the need to focus. Studies for my first degree might have benefited from a little more focus. I was certainly capable of achieving higher results. Student life in our day was a lot more than that. I mentioned in the Foreword that the Vice-Chancellor had exhorted us at Orientation: "Of you, much is expected!" We were the 'one-in-forty' that made it to university. My university days were an opportunity for a rounded education, not only in music but also in the arts generally. Imagine being so fortunate as to have someone of the stature of David Malouf direct me in a University Dramatic Society play!

Had it not been for my brother John, I would not have discovered all of this. He broadened my focus guided by his own educational background in the classics. He took me beyond what is now called 'tunes'. How I hate that word – a quintessential American trivialization justified by the fact that it makes money.

The essence

In the chapter 'The end of Innocence' I talked about being stripped down to the 'essence'. For me that would be the cultural core which developed in me through music – not 'tunes' or, even worse, stuff that should really be called 'noise'.

I don't own that cultural core; it has been handed down to each one of us from earlier generations. And I believe it is the steel that underpins western achievements such as man reaching the moon.

Our society risks rotting away from the core if we are not prepared to affirm and strengthen our underpinnings. For some, that would be religion. For me, it is the hundreds of years of cultural development. But I needed a guide, Bro John, to help me break through the teenage prejudices that would have cut me off from all of that which subsequently has so enriched my whole life.

I admire the parents who can see beyond the distractions of the local idiosyncrasies and direct their kids into 'the main game'. That could be learning ballet or learning the piano. Or it could be resisting the hype of the local game (AFL) which is, let's face it, about as popular outside Australia as the Proton car is outside of Malaysia!

Though I'll be condemned for 'elitism', I really want to stress to Riley, Jasper, Tristan, Oliver, Zander, Libby, Avi, Anu and Mika to engage with those cultural foundations. Don't be distracted by what others are doing, just quietly pursue what I call the 'main game'. I recently discovered that the famous Australian pianist, writer and festival director, Anna Goldsworthy shares my opinion:

> "Asian parents value the study of music as a discipline and craft: without exception, students of Asian background have dominated every Australian piano competition I have adjudicated over the past decade".

> "Finland is a world leader in music education for children, with the value of music enshrined in the curriculum in government legislation".

> "Countless studies reveal that music education will improve our children's executive function, social ability, literacy, numeracy, concentration, brain function, fine motor skills, creative thinking, working memory, study habits and even their self-esteem".

Time to Think

Ever noticed that you get some of your best ideas under the shower in the morning? Could it be the warm water on the head? There's more to it than that. It's the five minutes or so when you are *not* tweeting, *not* instagramming, *not* cramming your head with an iPod.

We need processing time – not continuous inputs. We need time to be bored, time to let our minds wander. (See **On Boredom**) Samantha has shared her insights on this in many discussions we have had about the creative process.

The German Philosopher Marin Heidegger in his 100 page treatise on boredom defined the most extensive philosophical treatment ever of the subject. He focused on waiting at railway stations in particular as a major context of boredom.

> "Profound boredom, drifting here and there in the abysses of our existence like a muffling fog, removes all things and men and oneself along with it into a remarkable indifference. This boredom reveals being as a whole."
>
> "Common passive ways to escape boredom are to sleep or to think creative thoughts (daydream). Boredom also plays a role in existentialist thought. In contexts where one is confined, spatially or otherwise, boredom may be met with various religious activities. Boredom may be taken as the essential human condition to which God, wisdom, or morality are the ultimate answers".

That opportunity for existentialist thought is, I guess, what underlies the whole concept of a retreat, or a Monastery. I wonder whether Twitter or Facebook are allowed in a Monastery?

Hugh Fraser eulogising father Malcolm quotes Sheila Hancock from *"My Life with John Thaw"*

"It matters to have trodden the earth proudly, not arrogantly, but on feet that aren't afraid to stand their ground and move quickly when the need arises."

"It matters that your eyes have been on the object always, aware of its drift but not caught up in it."

"It matters that we were young together, and that you never lost the instincts and intuitions of a pioneer."

"It matters that you have been brave when retreat would have been easier."

"It matters that, in many places and at many times, you have made a difference."

"Your laugh has mattered. Your love has mattered."

"Above all, it matters that you have been loved. Nothing else matters."

The last word is from Mikhail Gorbachev of his beloved wife Raisa

Raisa shared my birthday, January 5th 1932, nine years prior to mine in 1941. Some of you have heard me relate this story from *The Economist*.

Beloved husband Mikhail surprised the communists by choosing a Russian Orthodox Church outside of Moscow – one that enabled the casket to be physically carried to the place of internment over a gravel pathway.

He allowed the mutterings of the Priests but, other than that, he asked mourners to preserve the silence. The only other sounds heard were the sobbing, the crunch of the gravel underfoot as the casket was borne to the grave, and the sound of the earth hitting the top of the coffin. Each mourner, having their own personal relationship with the deceased, was invited, in their own personal way: *Contemplate the loss!*

John Fitzgerald Kennedy

Imagine the brief: 50,000 private citizens of Dallas Texas have donated a total of $200,000 for a memorial to their beloved, assassinated President. A square of land, not 200 yards from the point where he was so brutally slain, has been set aside by the city.

Famed American architect and Kennedy family friend Philip Johnson proposed:

> "a place of quiet refuge, an enclosed place of thought and contemplation separated from the city around, but near the sky and earth."

> "the idea of going into an empty room with nothing provided to you, except these three words: John Fitzgerald Kennedy, to think about the slain president. I think that's a very moving image."

> "it would be left to the visitors to find their own meaning."

Again, Phillip Johnson is saying: *Contemplate the Loss!*

Jacqueline Kennedy approved the design of the memorial.

It is a square, roofless room, 9.1 m tall, 15 by 15 m square, with two narrow openings facing north and south. The walls consist of 72 white precast concrete panels each ending 80 cms above ground. Columns act as legs that support the monument each ending in a light fixture. At night, the lights create the illusion that the structure is supported by the light itself.

My generation were the first spared close experience of the scars of World War II – we were too young to understand. For most of us, the worse thing we suffered was war rationing (see **Childhood cameo: Austerity morphs into Abundance**)

It was the assassination of our hero, President John Kennedy in 1963 when many of us experienced profound grief for the first time – the unbelievability that this could even happen. [More recently, the 9/11 atrocity evoked the same absolute disbelief that such a thing could even happen and the associated profound shake to one's faith in human nature].

Unsurprisingly, in trips to USA, we've made visits to key sites such as JFK's grave in Arlington Cemetery, as early as 1967. In 2018, Ann and I stood at the reflective pools Ground Zero New York and, stopping-off on our way home. we visited Dallas Texas and the Philip Johnson Memorial to JFK. We reflected.

The Music

Joni Mitchell, unlike many modern travellers observed by Alain de Botton (see back cover), **did** look out of the plane window:

> "I was reading *Henderson the Rain King* on a plane and, early in the book, Henderson is also up in a plane. He's on his way to Africa and he looks down and sees these clouds.
>
> I put down the book, looked out the window and saw clouds too, and I immediately started writing the song."

> Rows and flows of angel hair
> And ice cream castles in the air
> And feather canyons everywhere
> Looked at clouds that way
>
> But now they only block the sun
> They rain and they snow on everyone
> So many things I would have done
> But clouds got in my way
>
> I've looked at clouds from both sides now
> From up and down and still somehow
> It's cloud illusions I recall
> I really don't know clouds at all
>
> I've looked at life from both sides now
> From win and lose and still somehow
> It's life's illusions I recall
> I really don't know life at all

www.ingramcontent.com/pod-product-compliance
Lightning Source LLC
Chambersburg PA
CBHW060647150426
42811CB00086B/2454/J